PRAISE FOR L.A. WRITERS' LAB'S
90-DAY MEMOIR WORKSHOPS

"Writing a memoir is not a mere recitation of facts or a timeline of events. It's a jour- ney inside of yourself, coming to terms with the highs and lows and lessons every life teaches. It is that honest, raw, revelatory account that others will want to read and learn from. The 90-Day Memoir course from Al Watt is a masterful guided tour to that inner world, structured perfectly. And, amazingly to me, it ends with a mostly completed rough draft in just three months. That's something that many of us have spent years trying to accomplish. The secret is Al's empathy and teaching methods— asking his students to address the episodes they most want to resist. Few teachers can get their students to really think through the dark night of their soul and how that led to their eventual success and indeed transformation. Al insists he is not a therapist, and this writing course is not therapy. Well, for me it was full of deep personal revela- tions, helping me make sense of my life and to be able to write about it in ways that had always eluded me before. In short, I simply don't believe you can go wrong with this extraordinary teacher and his writing blueprint."

—**Bill Buzenberg, Journalist and Former Head of NPR News, Minnesota Public Radio, and the Center for Public Integrity**

"The workshop was without a doubt the key to getting my travel memoir about living with the poor in Vietnam out of a rut. Al is brilliant and has an uncanny ability to draw out the issues and angles you didn't know you had in you. It was also fascinating to hear the work of other writers and learn from Al's comments to them. I finished my book and had offers from two publishing houses."

—**Karin Esterhammer, author of** *So Happiness to Meet You*, **Prospect Park Books, Winner of the Nautilus Book Awards Silver Medal**

"I already had an MFA and I teach and direct a college creative writing program, but I really didn't have an organic understanding of story. Al's ability to merge intuition and structure is unique and invaluable. I was able to work through my outline-phobia because of the way he approached structure as a holistic approach, rather than a rigid box. Al encourages the writer to live within the questions of the story, not the answers."

—**Laraine Herring, author of** *Gathering Lights*, **Winner of the Barbara Deming Award for Women**

"Al Watt is extraordinary. Having had many powerful teachers, creative and other- wise, in my journey, I'm thankful to have had my share of amazing, often world class

instruction. Al is in a league all his own. His well-homed and well-earned mastery of the craft of writing, his awareness of the human condition, and his own very apparent evolution as a person, among many other qualities, coincide to create an experience like no other. If you have the opportunity to study with Al, don't miss it. I give both Al Watt and his workshops my highest recommendation."

—Robert Gant, actor *Queer As Folk*

"Al Watt is a story guru. Plain and simple. His writing prompts encourage you to dig deep and allow your subconscious to show up on the page. I'm always amazed at what I produce in Al's class and also how connected to my story he makes me feel. If you are willing to let go of plot, Al will help you find the heartbeat of your story. And then, he'll drill story structure into your head! I've taken a lot of writing classes, but working with Al provided the roadmap to complete my debut novel — the one I'd been thinking about writing for years, and now, finally, the first draft of a memoir, a story I never thought I could tell."

—Marcie Maxfield,
author of *Em's Awful Good Fortune, She Writes Press*

"It's the rare teacher who successfully does what they teach at a high level, while simultaneously inspiring others to do their best work. Al's encouragement, guidance, and insights into my manuscript were pivotal, compelling a deeper and truer exploration. He invited me to face all those things in myself that I would have preferred to keep secret. He never let me off the hook, but his notes always rang true as he gently challenged my ego to step out of the way. The result is a book I am proud of, and that I couldn't have imagined existing without his insight and skill."

—Arthur Dielhan,
author of *Get Out of Your Head, It's a Mess in There*

"This is the best class I've ever taken, and I've taken many in my time. I went from 'writing a memoir is impossible' to completing my first manuscript. Al has a genius method to unlock your subconscious and get you writing. I've been able to drop all my fears and get it done, which is remarkable."

—Sherold Barr, author of *Reach for More*

"I have two master's degrees, one from an Ivy League University, and I must say The 90 Day Memoir Workshop is one of the most thought provoking courses/workshops I have ever taken."

—Marty King

"Al Watt's marvelous courses have helped me in every aspect of writing. When you're thoroughly confused by plot and character, drop it all and run to L.A. Writers' Lab."

—Guinotte Wise,
Winner of the H. Palmer Hall Award, Pushcart Prize Nominee

"A line of heat and propulsion carries readers through the best memoirs. Al Watt, somewhat miraculously, has located all the levers and portals into that flow. With deep wisdom and compassion, he guides writers to the way it courses through their stories. A master technician, he's also part-mystic, part-soothsayer. Take his class, write your memoir and be transformed. What a ride!"

—Ann Marsh, award-winning investigative journalist

"Alan is the best writing instructor on the planet. He shines a light and steps out of the way. He honors the creative process and he respects the writer's soul. He is insightful and caring and generous. I feel lucky to have crossed paths with such an inspiring person."

— Anita Santiago

"Al's 90-Day Memoir Workshop is part structure journey, part shamanic tracking of self and part healing ceremony."

—Linda Kay Stevens

"A friend told me about Alan's online memoir writing course and she spoke so enthusiastically about it that I signed up, not really knowing what to expect. First, I must say, Alan makes this substantive course very affordable to everyone, which says a lot about the kind of person Alan is. I've been a writer all my adult life, but I'd never considered writing a memoir. Alan is an exceptional teacher/mentor who knows his subject well—but beyond that he is an intuitive, compassionate person who allows everyone to feel safe, accepted and "heard." He creates an environment that is encouraging and motivating. It has been a transformative experience, not just as a writer, but on a very personal level, and that is because of Alan's ability to work within the complexities of a very diverse group of people and make everyone feel unconditionally accepted and encouraged throughout the writing process."

—Carol DeFina

Also by Alan Watt

FICTION

Days Are Gone

Diamond Dogs

BOOKS ON WRITING

The 90-Day Novel

The 90-Day Rewrite

The 90-Day Screenplay

My First Novel, editor

the 90-day memoir®

by
Alan Watt

the
90-day
novel®
press

**the
90-day
novel®
press**

The 90-Day Memoir© Copyright 2023 by Alan Watt.

All rights reserved.

No part of this book may be reproduced in any form
without permission in writing from the publisher.

ISBN 978-1-937746-29-2

A publication of The 90-Day Novel® Press.
The 90-Day Memoir is a registered trademark
of The 90-Day Novel Press.

To my students.

To your bravery.

TABLE OF CONTENTS

PART ONE PROCESS AND PREPARATION

PART TWO THE OUTLINE EMERGES

PART THREE WRITING THE FIRST DRAFT

THE ENDING: **Your Protagonist Returns Home**

PART FOUR WRITING EXERCISES

PART FIVE CREATING AN OUTLINE

PART SIX SAMPLE OUTLINES

INTRODUCTION

MAKING THE IMPOSSIBLE *POSSIBLE*

Welcome to *The 90-Day Memoir*. This is a workbook. You can read it at the beach or keep it on your nightstand, but its real value will become apparent when you use it as a guide through the process of writing the story you've been wanting to tell.

The goal of memoir is to make the whole greater than the sum of its parts. We're talking about miracles here. Making the impossible possible. Fear turns to love. Ugliness is made beautiful. Misery transmutes, not into a tolerable situation, but into an ecstatic inner knowing.

Memoir has the power to take your reader on a journey that leads to a transformative experience. There is something you know, through your unique set of experiences, that can shed light on our common humanity. You are about to become a tour guide to our collective inner life, taking us on a trip that has the potential to free us from some limiting belief we have about ourselves or the world.

But here's the dilemma.

While your story already lives fully and completely within you, it doesn't exist entirely at the level of your conscious mind. At least, not yet. It resides somewhere in your subconscious. Yes, the facts of your life don't change, those endless series of anecdotes you whip out in therapy or murmur late at night on a shared pillow with your beloved — those stories you play over and refine as you search endlessly for an answer — those stories aren't going away. None of us can go back and rewrite our childhood. But through this process your relationship to past events can get reframed. In the same way a grain of sand agitates the oyster to become a pearl, *The 90-Day Memoir* offers a roadmap to transform facts into truth that can set you free.

This is the difference between journaling and memoir. Journaling is an attempt to make sense of some aspect of your life, while memoir is written from a place of understanding. *The 90-Day Memoir* offers a roadmap to making the personal *universal*. I've worked with hundreds of memoirists, and this is the point where most of them say: *"Um . . . maybe I'm not up to this."* While they're obviously familiar with the events from their life, they sometimes panic at the prospect of contextualizing these events into a coherent narrative. Some of my students have never written a story before, while others come to me as graduates of MFA programs where they felt bullied into conforming to their instructor's ideas of what it means to be a good writer.

Some of us have been fed this notion that to become a successful artist one must endure humiliation and allow your ego to shatter. I believe your ego is a necessary aspect of your Self, and without it, you may not have survived the things you are now compelled to write about. Your ego is not meant to be silenced — it is meant to be inquired into. In fact, you're not going to write your memoir from your conscious mind. Your *subconscious* is the seat of your genius. That is where your story resides, and so, that is where you will find it.

The 90-Day Memoir involves a process of *marrying the wildness of your imagination to the rigor of story structure.* Everything you imagine belongs in your story when you distill it to its nature. You can trust all of the disparate ideas and images that come to you, and I will guide you through the process of distilling this material into a story with a beginning, middle, and end.

As you do this work you may discover that your heart is opening, and that you're seeing your story, and yourself, in a new way. You may discover compassion you didn't know existed, or rage at allowing boundaries to be crossed, or grief at losses you had convinced yourself were no big deal. You may discover that this work changes your life in subtle and not so subtle ways. The key to remember is that you're not the author of your memoir, at least not your conscious self. You're the channel for the story that wants to be told through you.

The 90-Day Memoir is not an academic textbook. There is no dogma, no rules — only principles. I believe the desire to write is connected to the desire to evolve. While your external success is never guaranteed, when you take the risk of allowing the thrill of creation to be your reward, the benefits often exceed anything you can imagine. When you concern yourself with the result, you're sometimes less inclined to visit those dark crevices of your psyche where the juicy stuff resides.

Do you find yourself wondering, *Should I bother writing this thing? Will anyone be interested in what I have to say?* If so, then you're bypassing the impulse to express. In other words, you're listening to a voice that isn't yours. This is a critical voice that may, ironically, be trying to protect you from getting hurt. You don't have to ignore it or silence it; you can simply be curious about it and notice where it lives in your story.

You're on a search for the truth that may feel, at least in the beginning, like some vague unnamable tugging at the edges of your consciousness, or like the shadows of passing cars on your wall as you lie awake at night. And perhaps the greatest obstacle: *What if I'm wrong? What if my truth is inaccurate? What if my loved ones disagree?* And perhaps underneath all of this: *What if I'm abandoned?* Your mind does a number on you when you start to dig. It seems we're hard-wired to stick with the safe and familiar. But you know something isn't right. You sense you're carrying a burden that doesn't belong to you, some psychic detritus — it's ancestral, this unnamable dread. And you fear that to write it down might, in some way, be disloyal.

You fear you're breaking *the oath*.

But what if your disloyalty is not to your loved ones, but to a shared lie, a limiting belief you've been carrying about yourself and the world? You know in your heart that truth is your birthright, but you're beginning to glimpse the fact that there's a cost to this freedom. It demands risk. It demands betraying the lie. Your mind searches for a way around this cold fact. (Have you found one yet?)

Have you ever noticed that while the facts of your life are indisputable, your *story* of them is evolving, almost like you carry within your heart your very own Rashomon. Something that seemed unforgivable might shift, while a casual slight opens your eyes to patterns of deceit you've spent a lifetime trying to ignore.

What if you allowed yourself to connect to your heart's desire, that place that didn't hide in denial, didn't self-sabotage, was able to speak your truth? The goal of writing a memoir is to develop a coherent narrative for some aspect of your life. Through this process, you may discover that you possess a power and wisdom that you previously believed was unimaginable.

This is not a book about how to get published. It's a guide designed to take you on a journey to meet your truest Self. The journey is thrilling and fun, and sometimes scary, but you're not alone. Many have gone before you. And whether you're working through this book in solitude or with a group of your writer friends, I'm going to guide you each step of the way.

AL WATT

P.S. — If you're looking for additional resources and support, just go to lawriterslab.com/resources/ to find a guided story structure meditation, downloadable worksheets, sample outlines, and a growing library of videos and other materials you may find useful.

PART ONE

process and preparation

AN OVERVIEW OF THE PROCESS

Being a writer is not something you are, it's something you do. Anyone who writes stories will tell you that, on some level, the process is mysterious, even humbling. They didn't *write it*. It was written *through them*. They didn't figure it all out, and then scribble it down. Here's what they did, whether consciously or not: They accepted that they weren't the author, but the channel, and then they followed their passion and curiosity, they followed their delight, their mischief, their rage and their grief, and line by line, they listened to their ideal reader who sat quietly in the corner, saying *tell me more*, and they trusted that these words, as they continued to accumulate, were leading somewhere, and gradually they discovered that these words that sometimes seemed foreign, confusing, mysterious and even contradictory and heretical, were guiding them to a truth.

There's no such thing as a *writer*; there's just the act of putting words on the page. Over the next 90 days I encourage you to divest yourself of trying to become a noun so you can lose yourself in the verb.

SO WHY DID I HAVE TROUBLE BEFORE?

Have you been working on your memoir for a decade? Longer perhaps? Is it something you occasionally fish out of your drawer or computer file and mull over, fiddle with, then put away for another year or so? Do you sometimes just stare at it, wondering what it all means? Does it feel anecdotal, like a series of disconnected stories that don't really build in meaning? Is it interesting perhaps, but not really thematically coherent? *The 90-Day Memoir* is going to guide you through a process of *marrying the wildness of your imagination to the rigor of story structure.*

This book speaks unabashedly to your heart, not for sentimental reasons, but because that is where your story resides. *Why you write* is at least as important as *what you write*. Grammar, punctuation and syntax are unimportant in your first draft. The goal of *The 90-Day Memoir* is to get the story down. Through this process we're going to keep your left-brain busy with tasks and prompts so your right-brain (your creative side) can do the heavy lifting and surprise you on the page.

IMAGINING THE WORLD OF YOUR STORY

The first step in *The 90-Day Memoir* process is simply imagining the world of your story. You may have noticed that when you attempt to plot out your story, you tend to get stuck, mired in your idea of what the story ought to be. It's not that your idea is wrong, but that it is not the whole story. The truth resides in your subconscious, and when you allow your subconscious a period of time to play without imposing a framework, you begin to see your story in a more dynamic way. Imagining the world simply involves getting all of the images, ideas, and fragments of dialogue onto the page. You're going to spend the first four weeks doing daily writing exercises (it's sort of like downloading your subconscious), so you have a rich well to draw from when you begin writing your first draft.

WRITING WITH YOUR NONDOMINANT HAND

Some of the exercises involve writing with your nondominant hand. (Don't panic, you're not going to be writing your memoir with your nondominant hand!)

But let me explain. We all have within us our true Self, an inner compass that we're aware of but often deny. We deny it in our attempts to get along, to be accepted, and even to survive. We tell ourselves we must be tougher, stronger, more vigilant. We rush through life, often denying our feelings and attacking life like a starving hiker gulping down a cheeseburger. Sometimes we become so busy trying to meet deadlines and obligations that we lose sight of our true self.

Over time, when we don't pay attention to this inner compass, we tend to stray off, lose connection, and betray ourselves in both small ways and large. Writing from your nondominant hand accesses a different part of your brain. It feels unfamiliar, forcing you to slow down, to become a beginner again. Your brain is always seeking efficiency, and when it is asked to adapt, it gets confused and takes you out of your preconceived perception of the world. The voice changes. It can be subtle, but also quite sudden and unexpected. This new person emerges, a voice you may have forgotten existed. This voice is you, your authentic Self.

Meeting your true self may begin tentatively, like two Golden Labs sniffing each other in the park. When you use your dominant hand, you are utilizing one hemisphere of your brain, but when you use your nondominant hand, you are accessing both hemispheres, forcing your logical mind to loosen its grip, and your creative self to emerge. You become connected to that tender state of curiosity and wonder. Writing with your nondominant hand is a way to bypass all of your preconceived notions of who you think you are and what you think your story is about.

When you write with your nondominant hand, you don't worry about penmanship. That isn't important. You're not going to show this to anyone. In fact, you don't even need to pay attention to the lines on the page. Ignore all rules of grammar and punctuation, and just write.

These exercises often release suppressed emotions. Take your time with it. Be gentle with yourself. If it feels like too much, take a break.

THE STRUCTURE QUESTIONS

Many artists resist the notion of story structure, believing that it somehow limits your imagination. Unfortunately, story structure is often taught by story analysts who approach structure as "plotting." The fact is that story structure has little to do with plotting, in fact, the structure that is being referred to is really the protagonist's inner journey toward transformation.

Story structure is a road map to your inner life that, when applied, can help guide you out of whatever struggle is besetting you. In other words, it's an immutable paradigm for a transformation of the spirit. In the same way Elizabeth Kübler-Ross identified the five stages of grief, the structure questions in Part Three are simply a series of questions that address the key stages in your protagonist's journey that lead them inexorably to freedom. These are not "plot" questions, but rather "experiential" questions, and are designed to invite images up from your subconscious at key points on your protagonist's path.

When you ask these questions over time, the framework of a story emerges. As you inquire, a beginning, middle, and ending begin to reveal themselves to you. Nothing is forced in this process. Some of the images that emerge may seem wildly disconnected from each other. The thing to remember is that your subconscious is the seat of your genius, and you will often only recognize the brilliantly constructed patterns after you have completed your first draft.

The structure questions open you up to your subconscious, that deep knowing place that bypasses your ego and stretches your imagination beyond the personal to the universal, places that might otherwise feel too dangerous and frightening to examine. You are being invited to reveal your true self by exploring the chains that kept you bound to your past, to discover that freedom is your birthright, and thus to claim a coherent narrative for some aspect of your life.

THE OUTLINE

As you explore the structure questions while continuing to imagine the world of your story, an outline begins to appear. Outlining is not simply plotting. In fact, it's helpful to remember that *character suggests plot*. By inquiring into the structure questions — which again, are connected to key experiences one always seems to go through in one's journey towards transformation — situations (plot) naturally emerge to support these experiences.

Your outline does not need to be a beat-by-beat account of the memoir you're about to write. There is surprise and mystery in this process. There is not a clear through-line yet, but there is a connection to the source, a sense that your characters are not merely functions of a plot, but are really, truly alive.

As you continue to imagine, you may begin to question things that you had simply taken for granted. "Why *did* I marry him?" "What was I thinking when I agreed to take in those seven kittens?"

As you do this work, you may even begin to discover things about yourself that you had taken for granted.

YOUR PROCESS IS VALID

There are no rules in *The 90-Day Memoir*. The creative process is mysterious, and while I'm providing you with a framework, there is tremendous leeway. This process, frankly, is about learning to trust yourself at the deepest level. Some memoirists require a thoroughly detailed outline, while others are more comfortable with a loose map from which to start.

As you move forward, you're going to find your own rhythm. How you apply these principles will be discovered and refined over the course of a lifetime.

WRITING THE FIRST DRAFT

You're going to spend the first four weeks imagining the world of your story and allowing an outline to emerge. Only then do you start writing your first draft. The goal is to begin the first draft with a basic confidence in where you're heading.

Are you expected to follow this outline? The irony is that when you begin the process with a roadmap, you discover that you can roam wherever you like. Once you begin, you will write your first draft quickly. Armed with a basic outline, you're going to write it all down before you have too much time to think. You're going to trust that the story lives fully within you, and you're going to be surprised at what emerges.

Remember this: it's impossible to have objectivity in the first draft. Don't judge your work. The prose is supposed to be messy. And please, don't show your pages to anyone as you work through your first draft! No one is supposed to read it yet.

PERMISSION TO WRITE POORLY

Your job as an artist is to build a body of work. When you drop your preconceptions about what good writing ought to look like and begin to trust the story that wants to be told through you, everything changes. Permission to write poorly does not lead to bad writing, but its opposite. You become a channel for the story that wants to be told through you. Your job is not to be impressive, but to reveal the truth on the page.

WRITING GROUPS

Are you thinking about assembling a group to work through this course together? Are you already part of a group? Every daily letter includes a writing group discussion topic to keep you connected.

Summoning the collective energy of a group can be very helpful. If you're going to do so, I'd like to offer some things to consider.

Don't read your first draft to each other while you're writing it. It's fine to share your responses to the writing exercises, but when you get into the first draft on Day 29, I want you to stay in your right-brain as much as possible, that place of joy, wonder, and curiosity. Having others read your work, and getting feedback, instantly puts you in rewrite mode. Don't show your writing to others until you have completed your first draft.

This is deep work, and we are visiting the tender spots of our psyche. It is going to bring up all sorts of stuff. Be kind and supportive with your fellow writers.

Is everyone committed? It's discouraging when you join a group and you're more excited than everyone else. On one hand, the group can carry you through the highs and lows of getting your first draft down, but if they're less committed, it can make it easier to give up if they stop showing up. It's worth having a discussion beforehand and laying down some ground rules. Make sure everyone is fully committed to doing this work, otherwise you may be better off doing it yourself.

Let's get started.

PREPARATION

You're going to spend about forty-five minutes doing some writing exercises that will help you to have a sense of where you're heading, and then you'll jump into *The 90-Day Memoir*.

Your goal with these exercises is to:

- Discover why you are uniquely qualified to write your story.
- Reframe your fears and use them as a way into your work.
- Develop a relationship to your protagonist's primal desire.
- Develop a relationship to the antagonistic forces in your story.
- Connect to your transformed self, so you have a sense of why this story wants to be told.

Are you feeling trepidatious? Are you considering putting down this book and watching funny cat videos?

Don't do it! Here's a quick exercise.

THE FEAR EXERCISE

Write for five minutes, as fast as you can, and list all the fears you have in writing your memoir. Nothing is too trivial. Be willing to write the forbidden.

Go!

Fantastic! You did it.

Now write that last fear you didn't feel like putting down on paper.

Good work!

So, why do we do this exercise? The first reason may be fairly obvious; by acknowledging your fears, they no longer exist solely in your subconscious. By making them conscious, you can start to work with them.

The second reason is that the fears you have in writing your memoir are *identical in nature* to the fears your protagonist has in your story. Consider this: on some level, you're always telling your story. If you interpret these fears literally, you may not get far with this exercise, but if you inquire into their nature, you'll begin to recognize all sorts of connections between yourself and your protagonist. (That's you!)

By exposing your fears, you're connecting to your vulnerability, your truth, your humanity. You're stripping away your societal mask and connecting to your primal self, that place that makes your work universally relatable. Ironically, it is your fears that make you uniquely qualified to write your story.

Many common fears include:

- I will fail
- I will succeed
- My family will hate me
- I'll lose my friends
- People will discover I'm weird
- I'll be abandoned
- I'll leave my spouse
- I'll expose my secrets
- I'll discover I'm a fraud

- I'll discover I'm a narcissist
- I'll discover I'm boring
- I'm wasting my time
- I won't do it right
- Nobody will care

This is a short list, but perhaps you can relate to some of these. Can you make a connection between your fears and the fears of your protagonist? Are you afraid that you're not up to this challenge, that you might fail (or succeed?), or that you will be *found out*? Have you noticed how your fears sometimes get very loud the moment you decide to commit to something new?

The thing to remember is that your fears aren't going away. If you wait, they'll only get louder. But if you give yourself permission to write from this raw, vulnerable place, your work becomes relatable. Be curious about your fears and remember this: You are uniquely qualified to write your memoir *because* of your fears. Memoirists often second-guess themselves. Don't think that because your mother-in-law still drives you nuts you have not experienced a transformation. If it still annoys you when she tells you how to live your life, that's because it's supposed to. A transformation does not mean you are forever liberated from negative human experiences. It simply means that you now see your situation in a new way.

WHAT IS YOUR STORY ABOUT?

At this point, you might have only the vaguest sense of what your story is about. Perhaps you're exploring an event from your life. It could be about coming out as gay to your homophobic family, or the struggles of being in a mixed-race marriage, or growing up as an autistic person during a time when neurodiversity was even more misunderstood than it is today, or maybe you want to explore your desire to protect your transgender child from a world of ignorance and hostility, or it could be about your struggle to individuate from your academic family and follow your creative ambitions, or maybe it's about your relationship with your dog, or the adventures of your final college year abroad, or your career in oral hygiene.

At this point, it doesn't matter how much of your story you know. This is a stream-of-consciousness exercise to help you explore. Write for five minutes and tell us what your story is about.

Great! Did you surprise yourself? What did you notice? Any insights?

Consider this: Oftentimes, story doesn't begin as a plot, or even a single memory. It often begins as a *feeling tone*, an ineffable impulse, an ache or yearning that wants to be expressed. This impulse is given life through the series of events that will eventually become your plot.

If you could distill your story into one word, what would it be? (Don't panic! Your word can change. We're just panning for gold.)

Here are some possible clues:

Freedom	Revenge	Survival
Meaning	Wholeness	Humility
Belonging	Connection	Beauty
Purpose	Success	Truth
Finding home	Motherhood	Destiny
Justice	Peace	Authenticity
Faith	Power	Courage
Honor	Self-Trust	Wisdom

Go ahead and write down your word.

If you wrote down *love*, consider this: Every story, in some way, is about a search for love. Love is the mystery that's always on the table. In fact, when you really examine stories, you'll see that the protagonist's journey often begins as a search for love outside of themselves, only to discover it's something they find within. Self-love can manifest itself in a myriad of ways, and each of these ways is a potential theme.

If your *theme* is the engine driving your story, then *love* is the fuel. It's the thing that makes the world go round.

Ask yourself this: "What will it *mean* when I get love?" And then, notice what arises. For instance, it could be: "When I'm loved, I will *belong*" or "When I'm loved, I'll be a *success*," or "When I'm loved, then I can finally be my authentic self."

This exercise can take you outside of your *idea* of your story, to the engine that is driving it. Through your memoir you'll discover that whatever it is you were seeking *out there* you will ultimately find *within*.

WHAT DO YOU WANT TO EXPRESS?

Story is the marriage of plot and theme. You might have a vague sense of *what happens*. Now I want you to be curious about *why it happens*. What do you want to express through your story? What do you want us to know? What do you want us to feel? Remember, memoir is a process of making the personal universal. What is it you want us to understand about ourselves?

Write for five minutes, as fast as you can, beginning with: "What I want to express through this story is . . ."

Go!

This is an exercise that helps you connect to your theme. Theme is not something you figure out intellectually prior to writing your first draft. This process is akin to a Polaroid coming into focus. The theme often begins as a primal impulse to express, and as you write it gradually comes into focus.

WANTS AND NEEDS

Here's a quick exercise to connect to the primal drive of your protagonist. In a word or a phrase, complete the following.

I want _____.

I need _____.

Notice that what we want is always outside of ourselves, and what we need is always within. What we want is an *idea*, and what we need is the *truth*.

Here are some examples:

WANT	NEED
I want to be free.	I need to speak up for myself.
I want to be successful.	I need to value myself.
I want connection.	I need to trust myself.
I want to be seen.	I need to see.

Notice that when you give yourself what you need, it becomes possible to have what you want . . . but *only if* what you want belongs in your life.

This exercise can offer a glimpse into your protagonist's "arc" — their journey from the beginning of the story to the end. We tend to make meaning out of our wants and desires. Through this story your protagonist is going to reframe their relationship to their want. For example: "*When I escape I will be free*," becomes "*When I speak up I will be free.*" Notice that our desires never go away. There is nothing wrong with our desires; but unless they get *reframed*, we will forever be in bondage to them.

THE DRAMATIC QUESTION

Is there something that holds great meaning for you, something you might even be willing to die for? Is it the rights of the under-privileged? Equality? Justice? Freedom of speech? Saving the plan-et? Living an authentic life? What do you believe in with such fero-cious conviction that nothing could sway you from fighting for it? Here's an exercise. Write for five minutes, beginning with: "*One thing I feel strongly about is . . .*"

Write as fast as you can. Do not lift your pen off the page. Re-member, it's just *one thing.* It's not a list! And *feel* is the operative word. Tell us what you *care deeply* about.

Go!

Well done!

By writing what you feel strongly about, you may notice a con-nection between *it* and the story you want tell.

Now, take what you just wrote and frame it as a single, arguable statement. Here's some recent examples from my workshops:

- "*I feel strongly that everyone's voice deserves to be heard.*"
- "*I feel strongly that children should be treated with respect.*"
- "*I feel strongly that drug addicts should be provided with clean needles.*"

Go ahead and distill what you just wrote to a single, arguable statement.

Do you see how what you feel strongly about is subjective (meaning it has an opposing argument)?

Here's some opposing argument examples:

- *"Not everyone's voice deserves to be heard. What about hate speech?"*
- *"Children should only be treated with respect when they behave."*
- *"Giving clean needles to drug addicts only makes it easier for them to keep getting high and potentially killing themselves."*

When you frame what you feel strongly about as an arguable statement, you may begin to glimpse the true conflict at the heart of your memoir. Your job as a storyteller is to play both sides of this argument with equal integrity. You must be curious about the other side's point of view, even if you find it reprehensible. Have you ever read a story where you felt like the author was pushing an agenda, trying to make you think or feel a certain way? It's frustrating, isn't it? You feel like you're being manipulated. When storytelling becomes polemic, you instantly rebel. At its heart, story is an argument, and it is only through this argument that we can be led to a deeper truth. These opposing arguments are the antagonistic forces in your story that will eventually be dramatized through characters in your memoir.

Go ahead and write down a possible opposing argument to your statement.

Do you see where this argument exists in one of your characters? Isn't that interesting? Can you be curious about this character and why they think and feel this way?

Story is not about right and wrong or good and bad. It is about cause and effect, action and consequence. Here's something to consider: *character suggests plot.* By embodying each of your character's experiences, plot naturally emerges to support them.

You don't have to figure out your story. As you inquire into the nature of your characters, images and ideas start to emerge. Without powerful opposing arguments, your antagonists will be two-dimensional and the conflict will flatline. And this is leading you to the dilemma at the heart of your story.

THE DILEMMA AT THE HEART OF YOUR STORY

Most human beings spend their lives trying to solve their problems. How can I get into college? Find a good job? Get married? Divorce this person? Quit my job? Go back to college? Reconcile with my ex?

What makes writers brave is that, on some level, they know that human beings are not really struggling with problems, but dilemmas. I think of a dilemma as a problem that can't be solved without creating a new problem.

Problems don't make for interesting stories. Let's say your protagonist gets a flat tire, he calls the Auto Club, and the guy comes and fixes his tire. Problem solved! Not an interesting story. But what if he gets a flat tire in the desert, and when the tow guy shows up, it's the guy who is sleeping with his wife? Now he has a dilemma. He wants to kill the man who is here to save his life. That could be an interesting story. Don't you want to see how the journey home forces your protagonist to *change?*

Think of it like this: Problems are *solved*, while dilemmas are *resolved* through a shift in perception. There are two ingredients to any dilemma:

1. A powerful desire.
2. A false belief.

Notice that every powerful desire (or primal drive) besetting you comes with its own dilemma.

For example:

- Faith: Show me physical proof, then I'll believe. (It's not faith if it requires physical proof.)
- Freedom: When I escape, then I'll be free. (Escaping can never lead to true freedom.)
- Intimacy: When I know I can trust you, then I'll reveal myself. (We can only explore the boundaries of our trust by taking the risk of revealing ourselves.)

Here's the other thing: When you succeed in resolving your dilemma, your situation changes, allowing you to explore the dilemma in a new way. This is why we have sequels! Our dilemmas never go away, they are simply invitations for us to continue to evolve.

Life is a struggle. The struggle never ends. As long as you're drawing breath, you will struggle with conflict at some level. There will always be tension. In other words, don't confuse transformation (the resolution to your dilemma) with some vaunted notion of enlightenment.

This isn't a bad thing; it's just a fact. You may try to remove the tension temporarily, perhaps medicate it with various forms of distraction, but you can never fully escape it. It is simply the divine discontent of being alive. Buddhists call it duality. Christians call it original sin. It's that thing that makes us uniquely human, and as storytellers dilemma is our stock in trade. This is what gives our stories a compelling narrative.

You don't have to invent a dilemma. It is baked into your story. It is only the specificity with which you explore it that will determine the depth and breadth of your story.

By connecting to your protagonist's dilemma, you are connecting to the source of your story. In fact, you are connecting to the elusive truth, the invisible cord that is driving your narrative from the very beginning to the very end.

Be curious about the dilemma at the heart of your story, and don't panic if you can't figure it out. It's more important to be curious and develop a relationship to it than it is to answer it. You're not looking for answers — you're looking for an alive relationship to the world of your story. If you're unsure, you can just explore an image that you have your story. It will likely be charged. You can be curious about the circumstances and ask yourself what the conflict is. The conflict will lead you to the heart of the dilemma.

Write for five minutes, exploring your protagonist's dilemma:

When you recognize that your protagonist doesn't have a problem, but rather a dilemma, your story begins to wake up. A dilemma is at the heart of every story, from Dr. Seuss to Shakespeare. It creates the narrative drive. Novice writers often want to control the process by believing their protagonist has a problem that is difficult to solve, but not impossible, while seasoned writers understand that it is only through the protagonist recognizing and accepting the impossibility of getting what they want that they can reframe their relationship to it.

When you inquire into the dilemma, you are literally tapping into a wellspring of images, ideas, and situations that, through the structure questions, will keep you thematically connected to your story. This is an organic process. You can't do it wrong. Through this process you are going to move from the general to the specific, by first creating an outline, and then, writing your first draft.

A FEW FINAL HINTS

1. Don't talk about your story to others. Talking about it dissipates the urgency to write it. Contain the energy. The only caveat to this is that if you are in a writers group and you are all working through this process together, it can be helpful.
2. Okay, you've talked about it. To everyone. They will ask you how it's going. Say nothing. Carry your story with you like a delicious secret. Don't tell your family that you're doing this. That is the surest way to become blocked.
3. Commit yourself to a time to write each day. We are creatures of habit.
4. I suggest writing two hours a day. Every day. Two hours will get you to the end.
5. Find a quiet place to work. Do this ahead of time.
6. Clear the decks. For the next 90 days don't get married, divorced, add a second floor to your house, or move across the country. Give yourself every opportunity to succeed.
7. Lastly, every writer who begins this workshop is terrified. You are not alone. Your fear is an indication that this story holds a tremendous amount of meaning for you. Through this process you are going to work with your fear, and I will guide you every step of the way.

What follows is a day-by-day guide designed to lead you to the end of your first draft.

Let's begin.

PART TWO

the 90-day memoir®

"While they were saying among themselves it cannot be done, it was done." — **HELEN KELLER**

WEEK 1

IMAGINING THE WORLD
OF YOUR STORY

This week is all about exploring moments from your life. This is a non-linear, right-brain process. If you allow your subconscious some time to explore without imposing any structural limitations, you will begin to make discoveries that will support the outlining process.

DAY 1

"The future belongs to those who believe in the beauty of their dreams."   —ELEANOR ROOSEVELT

TUNING IN

Dear Writer,

Welcome to The 90-Day Memoir. This week is all about tuning in, connecting to the story that lives within you. It is not your job to figure it out or to nail it all down, but just to inquire. The truth is, you are not the author of your memoir, but the channel. While your memoir already lives fully and completely within you, your idea of the story is not the whole story. The facts do not equal the truth, and so, through this process you're going to explore a series of events that will lead you to some kind of transformative experience.

The 90-Day Memoir is a process of trusting your subconscious to tell the story for you. Your subconscious is the seat of your genius. Genius is not a noun, it's a verb — something we all have access to. You're going to access it by keeping your left-brain busy with tasks it loves to do, so that your right-brain (your creative, non-linear side) can do the deep work of exhuming events from your life and contextualizing them into a coherent narrative that may perhaps surprise you.

Don't panic. The surprise is always, ultimately, a beautiful thing.

The purpose of story is to reveal a transformation, and through this process you will likely be transformed as well. If you show up and do the work each day, you are going to have a more coherent narrative for whatever events you're exploring. Through this process, you will likely be led to a greater sense of freedom.

Until tomorrow,
Al

WRITING EXERCISES FOR TODAY:

1) With your dominant hand, write for five minutes on each of the following prompts, beginning with:

- What I want to express through this story is . . .
- My story is about . . .
- You would never know this by looking at me but . . .
- My first love was . . .

2) With your nondominant hand, write an eight-minute stream-of-consciousness dialogue, between you and your inner self, beginning with: "How are you doing?" Some other possible questions might be: "What can I do for you?" "Tell me what you remember." Explore and listen and notice.

GROUP DISCUSSION TOPIC FOR TODAY

Did you have any breakthroughs or insights today? Are you seeing your story in a new way?

WEEK 1: THOUGHTS AND REMINDERS

- There are no rules to writing memoir. You cannot make a mistake in this process.
- Your story lives fully and completely within you, and you are uniquely qualified to tell it.

- This is a process of learning to trust your inner voice.
- The desire to write is connected to the desire to evolve. Your fears are a way into your story.
- The purpose of memoir is to reveal a transformation.
- Your protagonist has a dilemma. This is where the tension lies.
- Allow the thrill of creation to be your reward.

HOMEWORK FOR THE WEEK

1. Write for five minutes a day on each stream-of-consciousness exercise. Be willing to surprise yourself with what emerges.

2. Spend twenty minutes a day writing down memories from your past. Let them be random. Let your mind wander. You're not writing prose at this point. The goal is to fill the well with images, reflections, thoughts, and feelings. You'll notice that as you uncover memories, new ones emerge. You're exhuming events from your past and preparing to assemble an emotionally coherent narrative.

   For example: *I remember our family driving to Florida from Toronto, pulling a StarCraft trailer behind us. Four kids in the backseat. No seatbelts. Dad smoking with the windows up. Three days, trapped in the car. Running on the roof of our two-story house with my siblings while our babysitter, Bernadette, tried to get us down by spraying us with the garden hose. Sitting on the back step of our house, my dog, Sheba next to me. I'm 10. We're having a conversation, but I do most of the talking. I tell him my hopes and dreams. I'm either going to be a comedian or race mountain bikes. Maybe both. Taped pictures of Farrah Fawcett line the inside of my closet. I took "Are You There God? It's Me, Margaret." out of the library. My face burned with shame as I realized it was a girl's book about getting her period. Catholic shame. First confessions. Told the priest I had impure thoughts about Charlie's Angels. He asked for details.*

IMAGINING THE WORLD OF YOUR STORY

Spend at least twenty minutes each day this week remembering events from your life. They will typically be "charged" in some way, either positive or negative. This doesn't need to be done in chronological order. And while the events may not necessarily become part of your memoir, notice how one memory leads to the next, and how, over time, a recurring quest or yearning seems to appear. A "feeling tone" emerges that begins to suggest some sort of desire for resolution. As you continue with this exercise, you may discover that you are beginning to connect to your memoir's theme.

Try to take a nap each day. Even if it is just for five minutes after you write. While this work appears to be sedentary, it is also surprisingly exhausting and getting rest is essential. You are preparing to run a marathon.

DAY 2

"Freeing yourself was one thing; claiming ownership of that freed self was another."

—TONI MORRISON, *Beloved*

INTIMACY HANGOVER

Dear Writer,

Have you ever told someone you loved them and were met by a blank stare? You feel mortified, exposed, humiliated. You wonder, "How could I have been so vulnerable?" You want to hide, withdraw, take it back.

Yesterday you looked in the mirror and told yourself, "I love you," and now you're wondering if you can take it back.

Don't take it back.

Sometimes, in the process of meeting yourself, you begin to wonder whether or not this is worth it. You question your sanity, your memory, and begin a mental cost/benefit analysis on the efficacy of this endeavor. What if no one reads it? What if everyone reads it and they hate me? What if my family reads it and they disown me? What if I discover something about myself that is unforgivable? Why take the risk of telling my story if it will only lead to more heartache?

Remember, you never have to show this to anyone. That doesn't mean that you won't, but right now you are building a nest. You are preparing yourself for transformation. And while the person you are today may be feeling exposed, through this process you may discover that exposure is really just the shedding of a burden that was never yours to carry in the first place.

Until tomorrow,
Al

WRITING EXERCISES FOR TODAY:

1) Write for five minutes on each of the following prompts, beginning with:

- The message I got from my mother was . . .
- The message I got from my father was . . .
- What breaks my heart is . . .
- What brings me joy is . . .

2) With your nondominant hand, write an eight-minute stream-of-consciousness dialogue, between you and your inner self, beginning with: "How are you doing?" Some possible questions might be: "Tell me what I can do for you today?" Explore and listen and notice.

3) Continue writing for twenty minutes, exploring events from your life in point form.

4) Take a nap.

GROUP DISCUSSION TOPIC FOR TODAY

Did any self-doubt arise today? Are you questioning your story? Did you find yourself comparing your story to others?

DAY 3

"You own everything that happened to you. Tell your stories. If people wanted you to write warmly about them, they should have behaved better."

—ANNE LAMOTT

LOYALTY

Dear Writer,

Isn't it interesting how guilt emerges when you speak your truth? Why is it that standing up for yourself or setting a boundary brings with it a sense of shame? Have you ever been told you were "too sensitive," or that you should "get over it?" We internalize these messages until we arrive at a point where telling our truth feels like a betrayal.

And perhaps, on some level it is.

Except that what you're betraying is the status quo. You're betraying a lie that was passed down to you by your ancestors. The lie is this: keep your secrets and you'll be safe, pretend it didn't happen and it will go away, shut down your feelings and everything will be okay. And the obverse: if you tell your secrets then you'll be in danger, if you acknowledge the abusive behavior then you'll be punished, and if you open yourself to your feelings then the floodgates will open and you'll be reduced to an unending vale of tears.

It seems like a no-win situation. And yet, the truth is shrieking inside you. Despite your best efforts to quiet it, there's something demanding to be heard.

If all art is subversive, then memoir is perhaps more so. With fiction, you can hide behind your characters to some degree, but with memoir there's a certain dissonance that you can't outrun, because, after all, you are your protagonist.

The desire to write is really the desire to evolve, to resolve something you seek to understand. You want wholeness, freedom; you want to know and express yourself in some fundamental way. But as you begin to explore, you sense that your truth may disturb your sense of security.

In writing memoir, guilt often stands between you and your willingness to tell the truth. This is where writers sometimes get stuck. Writing your first draft is something you must do for yourself, because here's the paradox: when you write your first draft for yourself, you're more inclined to get to the truth. It's only by telling the undiluted truth that there can be any chance for transformation.

This process requires a certain amount of letting go, of faith. It might even feel, at least temporarily, disloyal. I tell my writers that memoir is an act of faith, but it's not an act of blind faith. You can put your faith in story structure because it will lead you beyond the facts of what happened to the underlying truth. Through your story, you're going to reframe your relationship to a series of events in your life and experience them in a new and transformed way. But if we don't experience the obstacles with you, there will be no context for your redemption.

Until tomorrow,
Al

WRITING EXERCISES FOR TODAY:

1) Write for five minutes on each of the following prompts, beginning with:

- I don't actually remember this, but I've been told that . . .
- I have a habit of . . .

- The last time I betrayed someone was when I . . .
- The last time I saved someone was when I . . .

2) With your nondominant hand, write an eight-minute stream-of-consciousness interview, between you and your inner self, beginning with: "What is your earliest memory?" "How did you feel about it?" Explore and listen and notice.

3) Continue writing for twenty minutes, exploring events from your life in point form.

GROUP DISCUSSION TOPIC FOR TODAY

Where do your loyalties lie? Are you loyal to your authentic self, or to some agreement you made that no longer rings true, if it ever even did? What are you afraid will happen if you speak your truth?

DAY 4

"The essential dilemma of my life is between my deep
desire to belong and my suspicion of belonging."
—JHUMPA LAHIRI

WANTS AND NEEDS

Dear Writer,

What we want is always outside of ourselves, while what we need is always within. Quickly finish the ending to these two sentences:

I want _____.
I need _____.

Notice that when you flip the want you get the need. For example:

I want to be free.
I need to stand up for myself.
When I stand up for myself I am free.

I want to be popular.
I need to find my tribe.
When I find my tribe, I am popular.

I want to be validated.
I need to accept myself.
When I accept myself, I discover that I am valid.

In your life, you tend to think that you're struggling with a problem, but in fact you're not — not really. What you're struggling with is a dilemma. A dilemma manifests itself as a problem that cannot be solved without creating a new problem.

BEGIN WITH THE END IN MIND

Why are you telling us this story? I've heard writers say, "How can I write my ending when I'm still living my life?" The ending of your memoir is not the end of your life (though it might feel like it.) It is the completion of a theme. The purpose of every story is to reveal a transformation. A transformation simply means a shift in perception.

What do we understand about your situation that we did not understand at the beginning? How do you reframe your relationship to your struggle in a way that allows you to transcend it and move on? The important question to continually return to is, "What is my story about?"

As you write your first draft, you may discover that the answer to this question shifts or changes. This is not a bad thing. Through this process you are going to begin to understand what you're trying to express. It's a journey. But by being curious about how your story ends, you will have a sense of the scope of the book, you'll have a sense of what you're trying to express, you'll have a sense of what the story means.

The ending of your book may be plot related, but it should also feel connected to what you're expressing. For example, if you're writing a coming-of-age memoir, the story could be about freedom, or the journey from innocence to wisdom, or it could be about justice. What does it mean to "come of age"? In plot terms it might be about a character's first love, or it might be about standing up for oneself, or it might be about losing one's innocence about how cruel or unfair life can be. Again, this is meaning. There is a reason that you are telling us this story. Until you have a sense of why you are telling us this story, you run the risk of merely journaling.

Until tomorrow,
Al

WRITING EXERCISES FOR TODAY:

1) Write for five minutes on each of the following prompts, beginning with:

- I feel the deepest sense of belonging when . . .
- Something I'm grateful to have lost is . . .
- Something I'm grateful to have found is . . .
- The nicest thing anyone ever said to me was . . .

2) With your nondominant hand, write an eight-minute stream-of-consciousness interview, between you and your inner self, beginning with: "When was the first time you cried?" Explore and listen and notice.

3) Continue writing for twenty minutes, exploring events from your life in point form.

GROUP DISCUSSION TOPIC FOR TODAY

Is this work making you tired? How are you feeling? Are you noticing anything different in your energy level? Are you getting enough rest?

DAY 5

"The unexamined life is not worth living."
                                    —SOCRATES

YOUR PROTAGONIST IS AN EXTREME

Dear Writer,

All sorts of fears can arise when you set out on a creative endeavor. There is a special fear with memoir however, because you're telling *your* story, and the desire to withhold information or temper the drama in order to protect yourself and others can actually lead to confusion for your reader. It is only through conflict or tension that meaning gets conveyed.

Notice how your protagonist (you) is an extreme through which you explore your theme. In Cheryl Strayed's memoir, *Wild,* she is going to walk the Pacific Crest Trail, a thousand miles of wilderness, to find herself. In *The Men We Reaped*, Jesmyn Ward explores the loss of five African American men in her life who died within the course of four years, confronting the injustice of poverty and racial inequality and how it leads to tragic consequences. In Canadian journalist Melissa Fungs' memoir, *Under an Afghan Sky*, she tells the story of how, while on assignment in Afghanistan she was kidnapped and held captive in a hole in the ground for twenty-eight days where she was occasionally beaten and repeatedly raped. Everyone can relate to the experience of feeling lost, or being a witness of injustice, or like they were being held hostage in some way, but notice how these three authors are exploring their themes through extreme circumstances. If they can come out the other side and make meaning of their struggle, then perhaps there is hope for us.

So notice how, in some way, your protagonist is an extreme. This doesn't mean that you have to have experienced terrible loss or abuse in order to have a story, but to illustrate a dynamic journey for your protagonist we must experience an obstacle that has been overcome.

Ask yourself what your story is about. Distill it to a word or a phrase, and make it primal. Here are some possibilities to consider, but feel free to find your own:

Acceptance	Connection
Ambition	Meaning (Who am I?)
Purpose	Survival
Freedom	Justice
Honor	Success
Validation	Belonging

As you continue scribbling down events from your life, notice how each event presents a clue to what you're seeking. It's not so much the event, but the meaning you ascribe to the event that really matters. As you explore, you will discover a sort of quiet yearning through all of these seemingly disparate events. You may also notice that you are seeking many different things simultaneously. One of them is going to start to bubble to the surface, to take precedence, and this will gradually become your theme, the lens through which your story is told. It is not important to answer the question of your theme, but to be gently curious.

Until tomorrow,
Al

WRITING EXERCISES FOR TODAY:

1) Write for five minutes on each of the following prompts, beginning with:

- I'm always shocked to hear that . . .
- I'm too hard on myself for . . .
- My family wishes that I would . . .
- Something I wish I could forget is . . .

2) With your nondominant hand, write an eight-minute stream-of-consciousness interview, between you and your inner self, beginning with: "Tell me when your feelings got hurt." Explore and listen and notice.

3) Continue writing for twenty minutes, exploring events from your life in point form.

GROUP DISCUSSION TOPIC FOR TODAY

Are you noticing anything different in your relationships? Are you feeling protective of your writing time?

DAY 6

*"Yes, I am a dreamer. For a dreamer is one who can
only find his way by moonlight, and his punishment
is that he sees the dawn before the rest of the world."*

—OSCAR WILDE

TRUST YOUR IMAGINATION

Dear Writer,

I sometimes joke that the only difference between writing class and
therapy is that in writing class you are guaranteed a transformation. All you have to do is imagine it. Of course, I'm not denigrat-
ing therapy, but sometimes one goes to therapy to solve a problem,
when what they're really struggling with is a dilemma. The major
issues in our lives are only resolved through seeing our situation in
a new way.

By getting a wider perspective, you begin to glimpse possibilities that previously seemed unimaginable.

Notice the dilemma at the heart of your story, this seemingly
intractable conundrum besetting your protagonist. And notice
how you continually approach the solution in the same way. You
approach the solution with absolute logic backed by years of evidence and experience, and yet, no matter how hard you try, the
outcome remains the same.

Rather than trying to solve the problem, imagine for a moment
that you are already free of the problem and begin to write down
your experience. How do you feel? How are you relating differ-

ently to the other characters in this drama, whether they are alive or dead? And what do you understand now that you didn't understand before? Take a risk and really imagine the depths of freedom and liberation you would experience, even if your logical brain is scoffing and saying, "You don't understand, this situation is different. This one is really impossible to be free from." At this point, it doesn't matter whether or not it is impossible to be free, but only that you are willing to imagine it.

Until tomorrow,
Al

WRITING EXERCISES FOR TODAY:

1) Write for five minutes on each of the following prompts, beginning with:

- Imagine yourself transformed at the end of your story . . .
- I have difficulty pretending that . . .
- The most alienating moment of my life was when . . .
- I no longer agree that . . .

2) With your nondominant hand, write an eight-minute stream-of-consciousness interview between you and your inner self, beginning with: "Tell me how clever you are." Explore and listen and notice.

3) Continue writing for twenty minutes, exploring events from your life in point form.

GROUP DISCUSSION TOPIC FOR TODAY

Are you noticing psychic coincidences? Did you overhear a conversation at the market that gave you an idea for your story? Do you see how you are naturally tuning into your story?

DAY 7

"Do you wish to be great? Then begin by being. Do you desire to construct a vast and lofty fabric? Think first about the foundations of humility. The higher your structure is to be, the deeper must be its foundation."   **—SAINT AUGUSTINE**

HUMILITY

Dear Writer,

A wise friend told me once that when you think you're humble, you're probably not. And that when you believe you're lacking humility, you're likely moving in the direction of having some. This is not a letter encouraging you to be humble. I suspect you already possess this quality.

The thing is, your humility can be challenged when you encounter fear, and this process can certainly bring that up. We tend to fear the unknown, and, as you may be discovering, the exercises tend to awaken our demons. So, how do you maintain humility, a sort of generous curiosity, in the midst of entrenched beliefs that you may have about yourself or the world?

Well, it's important to understand that your story lives fully and completely within you, and yet . . . your idea of your story is rarely the whole story — a humbling notion.

Modern psychologists tell us that memory is plastic and not particularly reliable in remembering events accurately. Even if you do, your interpretation of them will always be subjective.

Ironically, it is your humility, your willingness to step back from the heat of your memories, that allows you to explore the motives of the key players. This can offer you a wider perspective.

Humility doesn't mean that you dismiss abuse or manufacture compassion, but that you remain curious about the underlying meaning of the events you're exploring.

Until tomorrow,
Al

WRITING EXERCISE FOR TODAY:

1) Write for five minutes on each of the following prompts, beginning with:

- The secret I won't tell anyone is . . .
- The secret I don't tell myself . . . (This exercise is about how you are fundamentally okay, even when you don't allow yourself to see it.)
- My greatest accomplishment is . . .
- My childhood dream was . . .

2) With your nondominant hand, write an eight-minute stream-of-consciousness interview between you and your inner self, beginning with: "What was the biggest shock of your life?" Explore and listen and notice.

3) Continue writing for twenty minutes, exploring events from your life in point form.

GROUP DISCUSSION TOPIC FOR TODAY

Why are you writing your story? What is it that you want to express? Do you see how you are uniquely qualified to tell this story?

WEEK 2

STORY STRUCTURE

While continuing to imagine the world of your story, this week you will begin to explore an outline through inquiring into the structure questions (found in Part Four). Your relationship to the story is going to shift and grow. The key this week is to hold it all loosely.

DAY 8

"You can't write just anything. Your story needs structure."   —JAMES MCBRIDE

STORY STRUCTURE

Dear Writer,

There are no rules to structuring a memoir. There are as many ways to tell a story as there are memoirs. However, there is some craft involved; there are tools that will help you to develop a dynamic story. Through this process you are marrying the wildness of your imagination (those images, scenarios, ideas, and feelings) to the rigor of structure.

Story structure is not a formula, but rather, like the structure of a human cell, it contains within it the DNA of your fully realized self. Within each idea there exists a yearning, a quest for resolution. This yearning is the engine that drives your story.

Here's the opening of Joan Didion's memoir, *The Year of Magical Thinking*: "Life changes fast. Life changes in the instant. You sit down to dinner and life as you know it ends."

Nice! Shocking. Urgent. It grabs you. It elicits questions. But more than that, it wastes no time in telling us what the story is about. Ms. Didion does not tell us until the end of the chapter that her husband, the writer John Gregory Dunne, has died at the dinner table. While that is the inciting incident, the author knows that she must set the table for us first.

The story is not about the death of her husband (and, later on, her daughter) — that is the plot. Here the author understands that until she has provided us with the correct lens through which to see the story, i.e., "life changes in the instant," we will have no context for why she is telling us this story. Ms. Didion wants us to understand that this story is not simply about her grief experience, but it is also a warning that one day, perhaps very soon, her experience will be ours. It's a reminder of the fragile impermanence of life. This is a story about the experience of dealing with change.

As we begin to explore our story's structure, think in terms of how to set it up. As a reader, we need context. We need to know what we are being asked to care about.

Until tomorrow,
Al

WRITING EXERCISES FOR TODAY:

1) Write for five minutes on each of the following prompts, beginning with:

- The dilemma for my protagonist is . . .
- I feel trapped when . . .
- When I look in the mirror I see . . .
- Tomorrow I am going to . . .

2) With your nondominant hand, write an eight-minute stream-of-consciousness interview between you and your inner self, beginning with: "What have you come to understand?" Explore and listen and notice.

3) Continue writing for twenty minutes, exploring events from your life in point form.

GROUP DISCUSSION TOPIC FOR TODAY

Are you noticing any changes to your internal state? Are you feeling calmer? Angrier? More irritable?

WEEK 2: THOUGHTS AND REMINDERS

- The desire to write is connected to the desire to evolve. Trust whatever is emerging.

- As you inquire into the structure questions, hold the story loosely.

- Your story is leading you to where it wants to go.

- Be willing to surprise yourself. You know the facts of what happened, now be open to seeing it from a wider perspective.

- Your memory is valid.

HOMEWORK FOR THE WEEK

1. Write for five minutes a day on each stream-of-consciousness exercise. Be willing to surprise yourself with what emerges.

2. Spend twenty minutes a day writing down memories from your past. Let them be random. Let your mind wander. You're not writing prose at this point. The goal is to fill the well with images,

3. Spend at least twenty minutes a day exploring the structure questions found in Part Four. (Go to lawriterslab. com/resources for downloadable outline worksheets, a guided story structure meditation, and a library of free resources.)

DAY 9

"A mature society understands that at the heart of democracy is argument."   —SALMAN RUSHDIE

THESIS

Dear Writer,

Alchemy is an ancient brand of natural philosophy that involves the transmutation of base metals into "noble metals," primarily gold. Its other goal was to create an elixir for immortality.

The art of story is an alchemical process as well, in that we are exploring the collision of two seemingly disparate ideas in order to be led to a deeper truth. Freedom, for example: are you set free through escaping your situation or confronting it? Faith: is it blind trust or is it based on scientific evidence? The answer is both and neither. In other words, it is only through the struggle between two conflicting ideas that we are led to a new understanding of our internal struggle.

In the beginning of your memoir, you are setting up what the story is about by exploring this internal struggle. The plot — the events of your life — is merely the vehicle that carries your theme. If your story is about the desire to be free, you will notice that this struggle is alive in every moment of your story.

Ultimately, story is not about whether or not you will be free, but rather, how you reframe your relationship to what freedom means.

You want your memoir to build in meaning as it progresses by exploring this central dilemma. Notice how all of your characters in the story desire the same thing. This desire is primal. Ironically, it is this uniformity of desire that creates the conflict or tension in your story.

Until tomorrow,
Al

WRITING EXERCISES FOR TODAY:

1) Write for five minutes on each of the following prompts, beginning with:

- My biggest regret is . . .
- If you knew me before, you would have said . . .
- On my tombstone, I would like it to read . . .
- Tomorrow I am going to . . .

2) With your nondominant hand, write an eight-minute stream-of-consciousness interview between you and your inner self, beginning with: "What do you hate the most?" Explore and listen and notice.

3) Continue writing for twenty minutes, exploring events from your life in point form.

4) Begin exploring the four structure questions:
    Dilemma
    Inciting Incident
    Opposing Argument
    Decision/Reluctance

GROUP DISCUSSION TOPIC FOR TODAY

Are any blind spots getting revealed through this process?

DAY 10

"Remember, baby, don't never let a man mine you for your riches. Don't let him take a pickax to that treasure in your soul." —**CYNTHIA BOND,** *Ruby*

MYSTERY

Dear Writer,

Every memoir is a mystery. And every good mystery story begins with a crime. In the protagonist's journey, the crime is not necessarily an illegal act. It can be a betrayal of oneself.

Sometimes the crime is simply a state of ignorance that sets you out on a journey of self-discovery. This ignorance can be a lack of self-worth, some misperception of your true magnificence. This ignorance can be a function of your upbringing or your environment.

Think about the swan who believes she's an ugly duckling. Notice where you have been paddling around in waters where you didn't belong, not because you were "less than," but because you feared that speaking your truth might lead to isolation. Notice where you have spent countless hours and great energy trying to be seen by people who were incapable of seeing you. Notice how everything changed when you woke up to your true power.

Memoir is a mystery. You are combing through your memories in search of clues that will unearth the truth. These memories are often fragmented, and our transformation does not happen in a straight line. Two steps forward, one step back.

Remember, your memoir has worthy antagonists. There are

characters in your story that play their roles — these characters, while real, are also archetypes.

The key is to not hold too tightly to your suppositions, because through this process your perspective is going to widen.

In a mystery story, the detective is in search of the guilty party, but memoir isn't as simple as that. In our attempt to assess blame, we are often confronted with our own complicity, whether conscious or not.

In A.M. Homes' memoir, *The Mistress's Daughter*, she is contacted by her birth parents, and thus begins an investigation into the mystery of who she is and where she came from. Her identity is the theme, and thus a cat and mouse game ensues between her birth parents and herself, with all the parties trying to protect their sense of self-identity while at the same time yearning for reconnection, or at least, answers. The story explores the messy intersection of multiple lives, and how our struggle for identity gets passed down from one generation to the next.

In the end, the mystery in your memoir is rarely fully solved. Closure is one of those words used by psychologists to describe some imaginary unicorn of mental wellness. The truth is more complex and probably more interesting. It lies in some kind of weird grace, some ineffable bond we all share, wherein exposing our soft underbellies we can release ourselves and each other. The real truth is that we are never fully convicted or absolved, only mercifully released on our own recognizance.

Until tomorrow,
Al

WRITING EXERCISES FOR TODAY:

1) Write for five minutes on each of the following prompts, beginning with:

- I fear that when people look at me they see . . .
- One person I cannot stand is . . .
- My secret love is . . .
- I cannot wait for . . .

2) With your nondominant hand, write an eight-minute stream-of-consciousness interview between you and your inner self, beginning with: "I believe my purpose in life is to . . ." Explore and listen and notice.

3) Continue writing for twenty minutes, exploring events from your life in point form.

4) Continue exploring the structure questions.

GROUP DISCUSSION TOPIC FOR TODAY

Is your protagonist active? What are they *doing* to get what they want?

DAY 11

"You feel the shame, humiliation, and anger at being
just another victim of prejudice, and at the same time,
there's the nagging worry that . . . maybe you're just
no good."   —NINA SIMONE

SHAME

Dear Writer,

Shame is a brilliant way to keep yourself stuck. Shame is cunning and it can rear its head just as cleverly when things are going well as when it seems that your world is caving in.

Shame is our way of sabotaging ourselves so that we can remain in the familiar. Just when we are about to have a breakthrough, we find a reason to give up, to throw all of our good work away, to disappear into a fog of vagueness and despair, of learned helplessness. We convince ourselves that nobody cares, that nobody wants to help us, hence we don't reach out for support.

The antidote is not stiffening up, or going into the crash position. It is counter-intuitive, but it is your vulnerability, your honesty, your willingness to show your soft underbelly that connects you to the winners, to ones who will always have your back.

This world is broken in so many ways, but individually, there is an indestructible righteousness in so many of us, that when we're willing to express our truth, the universe rushes to our aid

— not to take care of us, but to give us the things we need to take care of ourselves.

Until tomorrow,
Al

WRITING EXERCISES FOR TODAY

1) Write for five minutes on each of the following prompts, beginning with:

- My attitude toward sex is . . .
- My philosophy on life is . . .
- My favorite thing to do is . . .
- The thought that keeps me up at night is . . .

2) With your nondominant hand, write an eight-minute stream-of-consciousness dialogue between you and your inner self, beginning with: "How can I comfort you?" Explore and listen and notice.
3) Continue writing for twenty minutes, exploring events from your life in point form.
4) Continue exploring the structure questions.

GROUP DISCUSSION TOPIC FOR TODAY

List three negative traits of your protagonist at the beginning of your story. Now list the opposite (positive) traits. Do you see where these positive traits live for your protagonist at the end of the story? Notice how *character suggests plot* — notice how this dynamic shift leads to a powerful ending to your story.

DAY 12

"You have been criticizing yourself for years and it hasn't worked. Try approving of yourself and see what happens."   **—LOUISE HAY**

YOUR BODY KNOWS THE TRUTH

Dear Writer,

Writing is a somatic experience. And while it appears to be sedentary work, it is really a contact sport. Writing is exultant, and it is exhausting. Except that the exhaustion creeps up on you. Quiet revelations come to light, illuminating things that perhaps you were hoping to avoid. You don't realize how tired you are until you put your pen down and realize that life's obligations haven't disappeared. The world is staring back at you wondering where you went.

Be gentle with yourself. Stay close to your work, and to any fellow writers in your circle. Support each other, and share your struggles. See how good it feels to be curious, to be vulnerable, to listen, to trust, and to be of service.

Until tomorrow,
Al

WRITING EXERCISES FOR TODAY:

1) Write for five minutes on each of the following prompts, beginning with:

- One day I am going to . . .
- The best thing I ever purchased was . . .
- My favorite memory is . . .
- My worst memory is . . .

2) With your nondominant hand, write an eight-minute stream-of-consciousness dialogue, between you and your inner self, beginning with: "What makes you feel free?" Explore and listen and notice.

3) Continue writing for twenty minutes, exploring events from your life in point form.

4) Continue exploring the structure questions.

GROUP DISCUSSION TOPIC FOR TODAY

Story Structure — Do you find yourself trying to figure out your plot? Or are you exploring the structure questions through your protagonist's experience?

DAY 13

"Home is where one starts from."   —T.S. ELIOT

HOME

Dear Writer,

There's nothing more primal than our quest for home. The dilemma is that our childhood homes may have been confusing, chaotic, or even violent. Whatever your experience, in our adult lives we often unconsciously attempt to recreate it in order to resolve it.

In her book *When Things Fall Apart*, Buddhist nun Pema Chodron suggests we're all addicts in one form or another, in that we're seeking something outside of ourselves to fill an inner void. Perhaps what we're drawn to is that particular "feeling tone" of our formative years, and while it may not have been ideal, at least it is familiar. We often experience a strong loyalty to home, adopting a sort of Stockholm Syndrome. Whether consciously or not, you keep the secrets you were raised on and hold fast to those values or belief systems, while simultaneously rebelling against them. You might complain about your parents, but heaven help the person who agrees with you.

There's something unnatural about turning your back on home. It is both a betrayal and a self-abandonment, and while it wasn't perfect, at least you survived. Right? Except, at some point, you start to realize that mere survival is an exhausting long-term life strategy. Somewhere inside, you hear the siren call of your soul. You wonder: What if there's a place where I'm not only tolerated but celebrated? What if my weirdness is actually an asset and not a liability? What if my thoughts and feelings actually matter?

Is it possible a place like this exists?

For some of us this notion can seem heretical, almost beyond belief, and so, we push it away. You can hear the call, but feel doubt. What if it isn't true? You fear you couldn't endure the disappointment of having your hopes dashed one more time. It seems easier, at least in the short run, to steel yourself from discomfort, to keep your secrets, to wear that cloak of propriety that keeps you safe but is also preventing you from experiencing the richness of life.

Yes, the pull of the familiar is strong. You may even believe there's no escape, that you're destined to orbit your familial dysfunction. Even when you make a little progress, a simple misunderstanding pulls you right back to the helplessness and despair of your upbringing. Why bother? How can you escape the deep roots of these unconscious patterns?

It's true that when you start writing your story, the gravitational pull can feel strong. But you can be like the first astronauts who escaped the earth's atmosphere and were suddenly thrust into a sea of quiet wonder, traveling at 17,000 miles an hour in eerie silence. They gazed down at this pale blue ball, and suddenly saw their home for what it was — a microscopic part of an infinite vastness. They were free to experience home with a new perspective, with a detachment and objectivity they didn't previously possess. Perhaps they saw their home simply as a place they came from, but that no longer defined them. Perhaps they connected to a much larger force, a force that was compassionate, loving, and always had their best interests at heart, a place of wisdom and truth, of stillness and self-trust.

I believe something extraordinary happens when you see your childhood home for what it was: it was simply the beginning of your journey, the beginning of a story that is being written by you, and no longer by your past.

Your true home is within. But first, you must choose it.

Until tomorrow,
Al

WRITING EXERCISES FOR TODAY:

1) Write for five minutes on each of the following prompts, beginning with:

- When I want to comfort myself, I remember . . .
- The closest I ever came to murder was when . . .
- The place I go when I don't want anyone to find me is . . .
- If you were to ask the closest person in my life who I am they would say . . .

2) With your nondominant hand, write an eight-minute stream-of-consciousness dialogue, between you and your inner self, beginning with: "Tell me the truth that I'm resisting about myself." Explore and listen and notice.

3) Continue writing for twenty minutes, exploring events from your life in point form.

4) Continue exploring the structure questions.

GROUP DISCUSSION TOPIC FOR TODAY

What does Al mean by *character suggests plot*?

DAY 14

"Love won't be tampered with, love won't go away.
Push it to one side and it creeps to the other."
—LOUISE ERDICH

CHOOSE LOVE

Dear Writer,

In every story, love is the mystery that is always on the table. In the beginning of your story, the question may appear to be a choice between loving and not loving. But perhaps you have already noticed that, in fact, you have no choice. And while love can be painful and messy and awkward and humiliating, the alternative is unbearable. It seems that as we each grow and evolve, we're constantly reframing our relationship to what love means.

Can you relate to this dilemma? *I want to belong (to feel connected and loved), yet not at the cost of losing myself.*

Do you see where this dilemma lives in your memoir?

Remember that love is an idea, it is subjective. When I ask writers what their protagonist wants in their memoir, they often say "love." While that is true, what we are really seeking is what we think love will provide, such as security, meaning, purpose, status, connection, validation, etc.

Notice where this lives in your story, because love is not your theme — love is the fuel that drives your theme. When you experience true love, you tap into that deep well of creative energy, an understanding that there is something beyond your own idea of how things ought to go.

Love changes us. When we experience love, it is the most obvious and undeniable experience. When we're scared or hurt, we question the existence of love and chastise ourselves for ever having taken such a risk and making ourselves so vulnerable.

Love defies logic. It makes you generous, it makes you sacrifice willingly, pulls rabbits out of hats, performs miracles on demand, and, as storytellers, it is the fabric through which you weave your tale. Love is brutal. It grabs you by the neck and forces you to look at things you've been refusing to admit to yourself. Love is madness — howling so hard your body shakes, tears staining your cheeks, unlocking something inside you until your heart cracks open against your will.

Love is my son's huge chestnut eyes staring straight into me unblinking over his oatmeal, while my wife chuckles at my silent terror, knowing I would sacrifice anything for this little monster.

Find the love in your story, dance with it, howl and scream and fight with it, so you can discover for yourself that it can never ever betray you. It is who you are in spite of all the nonsense you were told. Trust this place inside you that may be bruised and broken and numb, because it holds the key to your true power. When you finally submit to it, you will discover the ending to your story.

Until tomorrow,
Al

WRITING EXERCISES FOR TODAY:

1) Write for five minutes on each of the following prompts, beginning with:

- The truth I'm resisting about myself is . . .
- I would be crushed if anyone knew this about me . . .

- The thing I care most about is . . .
- Every time I think I'm going to get what I want, it seems that . . .

2) With your nondominant hand, write an eight-minute stream-of-consciousness dialogue, between you and your inner self, beginning with: "Tell me a secret." Explore and listen and notice.

3) Continue writing for twenty minutes, exploring events from your life in point form.

4) Continue exploring the structure questions.

GROUP DISCUSSION TOPIC FOR TODAY

Are you feeling distracted? Is anything coming up that you don't want to look at or admit?

WEEK 3

WHAT IS MY STORY ABOUT?

This week you are continuing to explore the world of your story, while allowing an outline to emerge. Through this exploration you may begin to glimpse that your protagonist's primal desire is offering you clues to a narrative throughline.

DAY 15

"Life is a constant struggle between being an individual and being a member of the community."

—**SHERMAN ALEXIE**

ANTITHESIS

Dear Writer,

As you explore the middle of your memoir, you are exploring the drama of your central dilemma played out. In the first act (or first section) of your story, you are setting up the world and the central struggle besetting you. In the second act (or the middle section) you have set out on some kind of quest (not necessarily a physical journey) to achieve some kind of goal.

On this quest, you are going to encounter all sorts of obstacles toward achieving your goal. Oftentimes on this journey, you will achieve some sort of early success. This is often a private moment of celebration where you believe that success is within reach, that it will be possible to achieve your dream or goal based on your current approach. This is an important moment in the journey because it provides context for what will ultimately become your dark night of the soul.

For example, perhaps you came from a broken home and believe that nobody will love you. The early success might be that you meet a mysterious character who shows interest in you. Do you see where an experience of hope or possibility might exist in your story?

Without this moment, there won't be a context for the next major moment in your memoir: the midpoint. This is an event in the middle of your story that forces you to commit fully to your goal. This moment often involves temptation. Can you see where you were tempted between what you desired and what was actually in your best interest? Do you see how you were pulled in two different directions at the same time?

The midpoint of your story moves you into the second half of your memoir where you may discover that the stakes are rising. You are beginning to suffer with regards to your desire. Perhaps you are considering giving up. Do you see how you are questioning whether or not you should have ever set out on this journey?

And finally, this experience of suffering leads to a dark night of the soul. Can you identify a moment in your story where it appears that all is lost, that you will never achieve your goal based on your current approach?

Until tomorrow,
Al

WRITING EXERCISES FOR TODAY:

1) Write for five minutes on each of the following prompts, beginning with:

- The answer to my problem I've been avoiding is . . .
- My worst defeat was when . . .
- I will finally rest when . . .
- My relationship to God is . . .

2) With your nondominant hand, write an eight-minute stream-of-consciousness dialogue, between you and your inner self, beginning with: "One thing I feel strongly about is." Explore and listen and notice.

3) Continue writing for twenty minutes, exploring events from your life in point form.

4) Explore these four structural elements in the middle of your story. Notice how all of these moments are connected by the same primal desire.

- An *early success*, or moment of false hope.
- A *point of no return* moment in your life.
- A moment where you *suffered* as a result of this point of no return.
- A moment when you eventually *surrender* or let go of the possibility of ever getting what you were seeking.

GROUP DISCUSSION TOPIC FOR TODAY

Do you find yourself trying to protect your protagonist, or any character? Are you willing to put your protagonist into conflict?

WEEK 3: THOUGHTS AND REMINDERS

- There are no rules to writing memoir. Your memoir may contain photographs, or be told in third person, or be a series of loosely connected short stories, or be narrated by your dead uncle. However you choose to express your experience is valid.
- Story structure is not a formula. At its most basic level, it involves three elements: desire, surrender, transformation.
- Story structure is a way of holding your characters accountable to universal truths.
- The structure questions invite your subconscious to organize all of your disparate ideas into a coherent narrative without having to sacrifice anything essential.
- Notice that what you feel strongly about (in today's exercise) will naturally find its way into your story. Notice also, that it is subjective, meaning it has an opposing argument. When you frame what you feel strongly about as a single arguable statement, and become curious about the opposing arguments, your story begins to come to life.

- The desire to write is connected to the desire to evolve; therefore, as you explore the opposing argument, you are led to deeper truths about the fundamental conflict in your story.
- All of your characters constellate around a central dilemma.
- Transformation simply means a shift in perception.
- A transformation cannot occur without powerful opposition. Story is alchemy—we only transform through great pressure.
- Resist the impulse to judge your characters or hold them in contempt. Rather, inquire into the reason for their choices.
- Notice how your protagonist and antagonists desire the same thing at their core though their approaches may differ wildly.

HOMEWORK FOR THE WEEK

1. Write for five minutes on each stream-of-consciousness exercise. Be willing to surprise yourself with what emerges.
2. Spend twenty minutes a day writing down memories from your past. Let them be random. Let your mind wander. You're not writing prose at this point. The goal is to fill the well with images,
3. Spend at least twenty minutes a day exploring the structure questions found in Part Four. (Go to lawriterslab. com/resources for downloadable outline worksheets, a guided story structure meditation, and a library of free resources.)

DAY 16

"We are imperfect mortal beings, aware of that mortality even as we push it away, failed by our very complication, so wired that when we mourn our losses we also mourn, for better or for worse, ourselves. As we were. As we are no longer. As we will one day not be at all."   —JOAN DIDION

SURRENDER

Dear Writer,

The purpose of your memoir is to reveal some sort of transformative experience for your reader. But there can be no transformation without surrender.

Through your story, you are on a quest. At some point on this journey, you are going to run into a brick wall, an impenetrable barrier that stands between yourself and your heart's desire. It will be a wrenching moment filled with shock and disbelief. You know this experience, even if you haven't yet married it to a particular event in your story.

This moment need not be some external loss like the death of a parent or the end of a marriage. It can just as easily be a seemingly small moment that heralds the death of a childlike fantasy, some timid hope that the world might not be quite as stark as it is. If you're lucky, this moment shatters your illusions, and you break through to the other side of something — you begin to glimpse the truth of your situation rather than the appearance of your situation.

Quickly, in a few words, write down this experience, this cry into the void. Don't intellectualize it. Make it primal. Here are some examples:

- All is lost.
- I'm all alone.
- Nobody loves me.
- Nobody sees me.
- Who am I?
- Help me.

This is the moment you die to your old identity. It's like vertigo. The room is spinning. You can't catch your breath. It feels like you're going to die. The thing with surrender is that there is nothing to do. You have run out of choices. You're at the end of the line. This is the moment you stop and everything falls silent. You hear the cheap plastic clock ticking on your bedside table, the distant cry of a child down the street who skinned their knee, the rise and fall of your breath as you sit in astonishment that somehow you're still here. And then the moment passes. You discover something within you that you had never known existed, a hidden power that becomes your ticket into the next phase in your journey.

This is the moment of rebirth, and there can be no rebirth without a death. You reach a point where you discover that it is impossible to achieve your goal based on your current approach, or your current identity. And while the facts of your situation are indisputable, your relationship to these facts suddenly flip. "All is lost" goes from being bad news to good news, because suddenly you no longer need to keep doing what you know will never work. You let go of what wasn't working, and you begin to ponder what might.

Until tomorrow,

Al

WRITING EXERCISES FOR TODAY:

Write for five minutes on each of the following prompts, beginning with:

- The defining moment of my life was when . . .
- The greatest love of my life was . . .
- The last time I remember laughing hard was when . . .
- The greatest thrill of my life was when . . .

2) With your nondominant hand, write an eight-minute stream-of-consciousness dialogue, between you and your inner self, beginning with: "Tell me about the first sound you ever heard." Explore and listen and notice.

3) Continue writing for twenty minutes, exploring events from your life in point form.

4) Explore these four structural elements in the middle of your story. Notice how all of these moments are connected by the same primal desire.

False Hope (i.e., Early Success)

Temptation

Suffering

Surrender

GROUP DISCUSSION TOPIC FOR TODAY

What is your favorite book? Who is your favorite author?

DAY 17

"One does not become enlightened by imagining figures of light, but by making the darkness conscious."   —CARL JUNG

CRY INTO THE VOID

Dear Writer,

There comes a point in your story when all is lost, when all of your hopes are dashed and you see nothing before you but darkness. It is only in this moment that you are able to begin to reframe your relationship to your true desire. It is in this moment that you suddenly become aware of your true nature, of the impermanence of life. Suddenly you see that your desires, while wholly logical on some level, are also quite ludicrous, and have in fact, been preventing you from experiencing your heart's desire.

As St. John of the Cross wrote in *Dark Night of the Soul*, "Now that I no longer desire all, I have it all without desire." It is in this moment that you realize that your quest to conquer the kingdom has prevented you from the simple truth that the kingdom dwells within. Ironically, it is only when you are brought to your knees that you can step into your true power and begin to see your situation in a new way.

Until tomorrow,
Al

WRITING EXERCISES FOR TODAY:

1) Write for five minutes on each of the following prompts, beginning with:

- I need to be forgiven for . . .
- If I could do one thing differently from my past it would be . . .
- My most painful memory is . . .
- If I were to tell the truth, the consequence would be . . .

2) With your nondominant hand, write an eight-minute stream-of-consciousness dialogue, between you and your inner self, beginning with: "Tell me about the one thing that you could never survive." Explore and listen and notice.

3) Continue writing for twenty minutes, exploring events from your life in point form.

4) Explore these four structural elements in the middle of your story. Notice how all of these moments are connected by the same primal desire.

False Hope (i.e. Early Success)

Temptation

Suffering

Surrender

GROUP DISCUSSION TOPIC FOR TODAY

Do you remember your first love? Do you see where this experience lives in your story?

DAY 18

"Humans need community, for our emotional health. We need connection, a sense of belonging. We are not built to thrive in isolation."

—ANN NAPOLITANO

CRISIS

Dear Writer,

Do you remember where you were when the towers came down? Do you remember the shock? The terror? Do you remember the need to reach out, to hold someone, to hold *onto* someone?

In our darkest moments, we reach out. It's almost involuntary, the need for reassurance and connection. Suddenly our petty differences vanish, and we grab the nearest stranger for comfort. It's primal.

The thing about the dark night of the soul, is that the person we are grabbing onto is our new self. The person we are seeking comfort from is a self that we previously did not know existed. Can you identify this moment in your story? Do you see this moment where you die to your old identity, where you can no longer tolerate the stress and anxiety of living the way you have been living? This is the moment that you can no longer continue in an abusive relationship, no longer continue hoping that someone will change, no longer continue abusing yourself with drugs and alcohol, no longer continue believing that one day the boss will acknowledge your good work.

The dark night of the soul is the moment you see the light, and you let go. You let go of the meaning that you previously made out of your goal, and you begin to forgive yourself for the absurd notion that your salvation lay somewhere out there. You begin for perhaps the first time, to glimpse your true power, and thus begin the journey back to your magnificent self.

Until tomorrow,
Al

WRITING EXERCISES FOR TODAY:

1) Write for five minutes on each of the following prompts, beginning with:

- I believe that (as your protagonist at the beginning of the story) . . .
- I now know it to be true that (as your protagonist at the end of the story) . . .
- Something I expect from others is . . .
- Something I expect from myself is . . .

2) With your nondominant hand, write an eight-minute stream-of-consciousness dialogue, between you and your inner self, beginning with: "Tell me what freedom looks like to you." Explore and listen and notice.

3) Continue writing for twenty minutes, exploring events from your life in point form.

4) Explore these four structural elements in the second act of your story. Notice how all of these moments are connected by the same primal desire.

False Hope (i.e. Early Success)

Temptation

Suffering

Surrender

GROUP DISCUSSION TOPIC FOR TODAY

What is your daily writing ritual?

DAY 19

"My Instagram doesn't cover my insecurities, my lack of self-confidence, that week I spent crying . . ."
—**AMANDA GORMAN,** National Youth Poet Laureate

WRITING THE FORBIDDEN

Dear Writer,

Notice how brave you are getting. Notice your curiosity, this quiet wonder that allows you to well with emotion without embarrassment, that allows you to smile for no reason, that allows you to remember a moment from your past that used to make you cringe, and now you chuckle.

When I was ten, my brother and I went to diving camp. Marnie Tatham owned the camp where she trained divers for the Canadian Olympic team. She had a big pond in her backyard in rural Ontario where she had constructed a variety of diving boards. She was a gorgeous woman who sat in a lawn chair with big movie star glasses and gave us instructions on all of our various diving boards.

One day, I was on the one meter board, right in front of her, and I had to pee. I was well trained, I never peed in the pool. In retrospect, I'm sure many of the divers pissed in her pond, but not me. Instead, I'd gotten out of the water after my dive and climbed back onto her board, where, dripping wet, and in my ten-year old brain, I decided that I would take a piss through my bathing suit. It felt like I was dripping with so much water that nobody would notice, until I looked down to see this river of piss gushing from my Speedo onto her diving board. I was mortified, but at ten you can't turn the tap off automatically, so there I was, pissing on her board, while Marnie just gazed back at me with a beatific smile.

For decades I would remember this moment and cringe, horrified, wishing I could take it back, almost as if I was reliving it simply to punish myself.

Then one day, I told my wife. To my surprise, she started to laugh. At first, I was shocked, and then I joined her. You know how laughter can become infectious, like you're feeding off each other? We were making lunch in the kitchen, and suddenly we're falling over ourselves, hysterical...and then the tears came. Something dislodged inside of me, a shame I had been unaware I was carrying.

By sharing our stories, we are no longer in bondage to them. This is the thrill of memoir, of reframing our experiences. What was painful or humiliating can become funny. And vice versa — what you used to deny through humor, can now be grieved.

Until tomorrow,
Al

WRITING EXERCISES FOR TODAY:

1) Write for five minutes on each of the following prompts, beginning with:

- My attitude toward money is . . .
- My attitude toward work is . . .
- My attitude toward alcohol is . . .
- My attitude toward marriage is . . .

2) With your nondominant hand, write an eight-minute stream-of-consciousness dialogue, between you and your inner self, beginning with: "Tell me your attitude toward love." Explore and listen and notice.

3) Continue writing for twenty minutes, exploring events from your life in point form.

4) Explore these four structural elements in the middle of your story. Notice how all of these moments are connected by the same primal desire.

False Hope (i.e. Early Success)
Temptation
Suffering
Surrender

GROUP DISCUSSION TOPIC FOR TODAY

Are you noticing how your antagonists continue to raise the stakes? Do you see how they want the same thing (at their core) that your protagonist wants?

DAY 20

"Great literature is simply language charged with meaning to the utmost degree."   —EZRA POUND

WHAT IS THIS THING ABOUT?

Dear Writer,

There's a difference between autobiography and memoir. Autobiography is typically an anecdotal recounting of events from one's life (often a famous person), while memoir usually explores a specific aspect of one's life, a special relationship perhaps, or a life-changing event. Regardless, what separates memoir from autobiography is that there is a thematic rigor to it that makes the personal universal. By dramatizing a set of experiences, something intimately personal is getting explored that is universally relatable.

Joan Didion examines the nature of grief in *The Year of Magical Thinking*. Elizabeth Gilbert goes on a quest for meaning in *Eat, Pray, Love*. Pat Conroy explores the nature of failure and loss in *My Losing Season*.

As you write, do you find yourself asking, *"What is this thing about?"* Does an answer emerge? Do thirty answers emerge and you're not sure which one to choose? Don't panic. Creating a memoir is a process of going from the general to the specific. It is less important to answer the question than it is to ask it. The answer can be fuzzy, even as you write your first draft — it might just be a "feeling tone," a yearning to make sense of something.

What is that *thing*?

What are you searching for?

Naming that thing can sometimes bring up deep emotions. It might feel embarrassing or even trite. You may have spent your entire life telling yourself that this thing shouldn't matter, that you ought to be over it, that it's not a big deal — but it is a big deal. And it's not going away by ignoring it.

What are you seeking? See if you can give it a name.

Write it down now.

ORDER OF EVENTS

As you continue inquiring into the structure questions are you feeling a bit stuck? Are the structure questions causing you to feel confused or like your life doesn't *conform* to them?

I want to offer you something to consider that might free you up: It is not just the stories we tell, but the order of events in which they are told that convey meaning. In other words, don't assume that because your life happened in chronological order that you must tell your story that way. In Tim O'Brien's novel/quasi-memoir, which is presented as a series of short stories with a main character named Tim, he moves around in time. The novel begins with his reflections of Vietnam, and it ends with a memory he had when he was a child.

Do not confuse story structure with chronology.

The structure you're exploring is *experiential*. You are identifying and exploring a set of experiences that may not have happened in chronological order. That's okay! Trust it. Memoir is not simply a recounting of events from your life, but the distillation of those events into a narrative that leads to a transformation. You're teaching us what it means to be human. If the whole is not greater than the sum of its parts, then it is merely reportage. Memoir is not simply about what happened, but *why it happened*. The order of events, the manner in which these events are conveyed, is surprisingly malleable. *The 90-Day Memoir* is a dialogue between you and your subconscious. Approach the structure questions as a set of experiences, and be open to the possibility that your narrative doesn't happen in a straight line.

Until tomorrow,
Al

WRITING EXERCISES FOR TODAY:

1) Write for five minutes on each of the following prompts, beginning with:

- I will die before I . . .
- If I had no fear, I would immediately . . .
- I will never forget the time that I . . .
- I could never live in a world where . . .

2) With your nondominant hand, write an eight-minute stream-of-consciousness dialogue, between you and your inner self, beginning with: "Tell me the most dangerous thing you ever did." Explore and listen and notice.

3) Write for twenty minutes, exploring in greater detail particular events from your life.

4) Explore these four structural elements in the middle of your story. Notice how all of these experiences are connected by the same primal desire.

False Hope (i.e. Early Success)
Temptation
Suffering
Surrender

GROUP DISCUSSION TOPIC FOR TODAY

What does Al mean by *make it primal* when he's talking about your protagonist's want?

DAY 21

"No person is your friend (or kin) who demands your silence, or denies your right to grow and be perceived as fully blossomed as you were intended. Or who belittles in any fashion the gifts you labor so to bring into the world."   **—Alice Walker**

ARCHETYPES

Dear Writer,

One of the challenges with memoir is that you can sometimes struggle to see beyond your idea of the characters in your story to their function in the story. Even in memoir your characters are functions of the dramatic question — archetypes — primal forces that constellate around your protagonist's dilemma. We dream in archetypes, and while our characters are real people, they are also functions of your dramatic question.

James McBride's memoir, *The Color of Water: A Black Man's Tribute to his White Mother* is a love letter to his mother who fled her Jewish Orthodox upbringing, married a black man, and raised twelve children who all went to college and some to graduate school.

When I was a boy I used to wonder where my mother came from, how she got on this earth. When I asked her where she was from, she would say, "God made me," and change the subject. When I asked her if she was white, she would say, "No, I'm light-skinned," and change the subject again.

It is a moving story that explores questions of identity and be-longing. McBride's mother attended school conferences where his teacher would ask, "Is your son adopted?" The title refers to the no-tion that we are not defined by the color of our skin, but by the val-ues we live by. Notice the dilemma inherent in the title – the pulse of this story arises from this shared desire (from all the characters) to find a sense of belonging.

As you explore the world of your story, notice how the people in your life each play a role. Notice how they all constellate around the dilemma. Whether it is connection or freedom or justice, notice how they all desire the same thing at their core — and notice how this uniformity of desire is the very thing that creates the conflict in your story. Let's say that you and your partner both want free-dom, however one of you believes that freedom comes from mak-ing millions of dollars while the other believes freedom comes from giving up all worldly possessions. Do you see the conflict? Do you see how story is not about whether or not your protagonist will get what they want, but rather get what they need? In other words, by the end of the story our understanding of freedom will (and must) get reframed as the result of these two people who deeply love each other battling things out in order to arrive at a deeper understand-ing of what freedom means.

Until tomorrow,
Al

WRITING EXERCISES FOR TODAY:

1) Write for five minutes on each of the following prompts, beginning with:

- The biggest risk I've ever taken is . . .
- The most uncomfortable thing I've ever revealed is . . .
- I secretly despise . . .
- I secretly lust after . . .

2) With your nondominant hand, write an eight-minute stream-of-consciousness dialogue, between you and your inner self, beginning with: "Tell me what you are most ashamed of." Explore and listen and notice.

3) Write for twenty minutes, exploring in greater detail particular events from your life.

4) Explore these four structural elements in the middle of your story. Notice how all of these experiences are connected by the same primal desire.

False Hope (i.e. Early Success)

Temptation

Suffering

Surrender

5) Notice how these four major story points are creating connective tissue. Be curious about how you get from one point to the next.

GROUP DISCUSSION TOPIC FOR TODAY

What's your latest breakthrough?

WEEK 4

GETTING MORE SPECIFIC

This week we will continue to explore the world of the
story and develop a specific outline. You may be getting itchy to start writing your first draft. (It's okay to start.
Everyone's process is different, and ultimately, this process
is guiding you to listen and trust yourself on a deeper level.)
My suggestion is to give yourself one more week to develop
a deeper sense of your story, and if you're bursting to start
writing, do it in conjunction with the story exploration.

DAY 22

"At fifteen life had taught me undeniably that surrender, in its place, was as honorable as resistance,
especially if one had no choice."
    —MAYA ANGELOU, *I Know Why the Caged Bird Sings*

TRANSFORMATION

Dear Writer,

The purpose of story is to reveal a transformation — and in order
to be transformed, we must first be willing to die to our old identity. Surrender is the initiation cost of transformation.

Sometimes we inch towards change. It can be difficult to imagine what is possible when we've spent our lives believing it wasn't.
And so, we tend to approach life like we need to try harder, push
harder, employ force to get the square nail into the round hole.

In Greek folklore, the phoenix is a bird that rises from the ashes
of its predecessor. It must die first in order to be reborn. In your
story, you're going to experience a death of sorts that leads you to
some kind of deeper understanding of your situation. You cannot
rise from the ashes of your former self until you've shed the limiting beliefs you hold about yourself or the world.

Einstein says, "You can't solve a problem at the same level of
consciousness that created the problem." In other words, it is literally impossible to make peace with your current struggle, be it your
controlling in-laws, your misogynistic boss, or your own addictive
impulses — based on your current approach. The reason is this:

You don't have a problem. You only think you do. What you have is a dilemma, and when you resolve your dilemma, your apparent problem suddenly vanishes.

Here's a quick exercise: Write for five minutes, imagining yourself transformed at the end of your memoir. Notice how you're relating differently to other characters at the end of your story than you were at the beginning. Be as specific as you can with this — and be curious about what you understand at the end that you didn't understand at the beginning.

Go!

Did you notice that everything you wrote sprang from an image? This exercise produces a goldmine of images for what precedes your protagonist's transformation at the end. Let's say, for example, that at end of the story you're relating differently to your mother — you're laughing together. Consider how you must show us earlier in the story how you are not speaking to each other. This may seem obvious, but if you don't show us the conflict, there will be no context for the new equilibrium.

Do this exercise for five minutes each day over the next week. It will help you uncover images and ideas that will start to fill out your outline in preparation for writing your first draft, which we'll start in one more week.

Until tomorrow,
Al

WRITING EXERCISES FOR TODAY:

1) Write for five minutes on each of the following prompts, beginning with:

- I couldn't live without . . .
- I resent . . .
- I am most envious of . . .
- I feel safest when . . .

2) With your nondominant hand, write an eight minute stream-of-consciousness dialogue, between you and your inner self, beginning with: "Tell me what you are tired of pretending." Explore and listen and notice.

3) Write for twenty minutes, exploring in greater detail particular events from your life.

4) Explore these four structural elements in the middle of your story. Notice how all of these experiences are connected by the same primal desire.

    False Hope (i.e. Early Success)

    Temptation

    Suffering

    Surrender

5) Notice how these four major story points are creating connective tissue. Be curious about how you get from one point to the next.

GROUP DISCUSSION TOPIC FOR TODAY

Are you feeling ready to start writing your first draft in a week?

WEEK 4: THOUGHTS AND REMINDERS

- Notice that your protagonist's primal desire never changes, although your approach to achieving it is always changing.

- Your protagonist's want is something outside of them, like validation, permission, connection. It is something over which they have no control. What your protagonist needs is within.

- Approach the structure questions as an opportunity to cull images for the story. Rather than worrying about where they fit, you can let yourself get excited that you are filling your well with images and ideas.

- The dilemma is personal to your protagonist, but universal to your reader.

- There's a difference between suffering and surrender. When your situation is difficult, you suffer. When it is impossible, you surrender.

HOMEWORK FOR THE WEEK

1. Write for five minutes a day on each stream-of-consciousness exercise. Be willing to surprise yourself with what emerges.

2. Spend twenty minutes a day writing down memories from your past. Let them be random. Let your mind wander. You're not writing prose at this point.

3. Continue exploring the structure questions. (Go to lawriterslab.com/resources for downloadable outline worksheets, a guided story structure meditation, and a library of free resources.)

DAY 23

"I believe it is the flaws that make us interesting, our backgrounds, the hardships."   —JANE GREEN

YOUR PROTAGONIST'S ARC/ INVESTIGATING THE FLAW

Dear Writer,

Human beings don't change . . . they grow.

We don't change, because there was nothing wrong with us to begin with. We are born perfect, just as every living thing is born perfect. There is no need to become better, in fact, it is that notion that likely causes most of our pain. Just as a sapling grows into a mighty oak tree, through this process of inquiry and investigation we shed everything that doesn't belong to us and we grow into the fullest expression of ourselves.

It is often in an attempt to improve your situation that you operate out of fear and make decisions based on your ego and not on your true needs. People often approach life as a process of adding on, rather than shedding that which is not us.

Perhaps through this process your goal is to shed all of the stuff that stands between your idea of who you are and your truest self. This takes work. It takes humility and curiosity, and the understanding that while you don't have all the answers, you have an inner compass that is guiding you to your True North. It whispers to you when you are moving off track.

Write down three negative character traits that you possess at the beginning of your memoir — three traits that are standing in the way of you living truthfully — and then across from each of them, write down the trait's opposite. Do you see where this new positive trait exists in your protagonist at the end of the story?

Here are some examples:

Ignorant	Wise	Petty
Compassionate	Distrustful	Trusting
Selfish	Generous	Lost
Free	Cynical	Optimistic
Despairing	Hopeful	Fearful
Loving	Judgmental	Curious
Timid	Open	Dishonest
Honest	Shut down	Vulnerable

Story is a journey. You begin in one spot and end up in a new spot. This is the promise that you make to your reader. Through your story, you are going to shed some false beliefs that you have about yourself or the world. You are going to grow and understand something that you didn't know before.

Until tomorrow,
Al

WRITING EXERCISE FOR TODAY:

1) Write for five minutes on each of the following prompts, beginning with:

- I wouldn't be upset if . . .
- I shouldn't feel this way, but . . .
- The most valuable thing I ever stole was . . .
- The worst crime I ever committed was . . .

2) With your nondominant hand, write an eight-minute stream-

of-consciousness dialogue, between you and your inner self, beginning with: "Tell me your most rebellious act." Explore and listen
and notice.

3) Write for twenty minutes, exploring in greater detail particular
events from your life.

4) Explore these four structural elements from the third act (final
section) of your story. Notice how all of these experiences are connected by the same primal desire.

- Accepting the reality of your situation, as opposed to the
  appearance of your situation.
- Taking action towards what you need, as opposed to what
  you want.
- Making a difficult choice between what you want and what
  you need.
- New equilibrium: What does it look like when you are returned home?

5) Notice how these four major story points are creating connective
tissue. Be curious about how you get from one point to the next.

GROUP DISCUSSION TOPIC FOR TODAY

Do you have a sense of your protagonist's *dark night of the soul*?

DAY 24

"Life at its best is a creative synthesis of opposites in fruitful harmony."
> —MARTIN LUTHER KING, JR.

SYNTHESIS

Dear Writer,

Story is expressed through a theme. Your theme is dramatized through your protagonist's dilemma — and this dilemma is experienced as a powerful desire and a false belief. For example: "I will be *free* when I *escape*," or "I will be *connected* when you *accept me*."

The plot of your story explores the question of whether or not you will solve your problem, e.g. "Will I escape?" or "Will I be accepted?" The theme explores whether or not you will resolve your dilemma, e.g. "Will I be free?" or "Will I experience connection?" It is the tension between this desire and this false belief that forces your protagonist on a journey where they reframe their relationship to their desire.

Ultimately, your reader doesn't really care if you get what you want, but they care deeply about whether or not you get what you need. Your need is primal. You cannot live without it.

In the final act of your story, the want and the need collide to reveal a deeper truth. The want and need are integrated or synthesized, and we understand your situation in a deeper way. In other words, it is only through an attempt to escape that I can reframe my relationship to what freedom actually means. Perhaps I discover that freedom doesn't lie beyond the bars of my prison, but within, and in accepting myself and taking responsibility for my crime, I may find a way to make my situation workable in the present.

Until tomorrow,
Al

WRITING EXERCISES FOR TODAY:

1) Write for five minutes on each of the following prompts, beginning with:

- Something I will never do again is . . .
- Something I don't feel like I'm allowed to say is . . .
- I have trouble reasoning with . . .
- I have unrealistic expectations of . . .

2) With your nondominant hand, write an eight-minute stream-of-consciousness dialogue, between you and your inner self, beginning with: "Have you ever felt lost?" Explore and listen and notice.
3) Write for twenty minutes, exploring in greater detail particular events from your life.
4) Explore these four structural elements from the third act (final section) of your story. Notice how all of these experiences are connected by the same primal desire.

- Accepting the reality of your situation as opposed to the appearance of your situation.
- Taking action towards what you need as opposed to what you want.
- Making a difficult choice between what you want and what you need.
- New equilibrium: What does it look like when you are returned home?

5) Notice how these four major story points are creating connective tissue. Be curious about how you get from one point to the next.

GROUP DISCUSSION TOPIC FOR TODAY

Do you have a sense of your protagonist *transformed*?

DAY 25

"But I have my life, I'm living it. It's twisted, ex-
hausting, uncertain, and full of guilt, but nonethe-
less, there's something there."
—**BANANA YOSHIMOTO**, *The Lake*

EXPLORING THE LANDSCAPE

Dear Writer,

This process is about making choices and holding them loosely. If it is feeling like a wild goose chase, then step back from your story and ask yourself what the one thing is that you know to be true. It might be a character, an image or an idea — but it is the one thing that you feel certain belongs in your story. From that point, start to ask yourself what the next thing is that you know to be true. Discovering your story is sort of like untangling a ball of yarn. As you do this, you will begin to identify where the tangle is.

Sometimes the problem we are trying to solve is not yet ready to be solved, and we can end up circling it indefinitely rather than investigating the thing that is ready to emerge. Keep holding onto the thing that you know to be true, and you will notice that you are being guided to a clearer narrative.

Also, remember that you are marrying the wildness of your imagination to the rigor of structure. All of these seemingly disparate images will gradually start to take on meaning when you apply the structure questions.

Until tomorrow,
Al

WRITING EXERCISES FOR TODAY

1) Write for five minutes on each of the following prompts, beginning with:

- I have unrealistic expectations of . . .
- I am far too understanding of . . .
- I refuse to believe that . . .
- Before I die, I am determined to . . .

2) With your nondominant hand, write an eight-minute stream-of-consciousness dialogue, between you and your inner self, beginning with: "Tell me what appalls you." Explore and listen and notice.

3) Write for twenty minutes, exploring in greater detail particular events from your life.

4) Explore these four structural elements from the third act (final section) of your story. Notice how all of these experiences are connected by the same primal desire.

- Accepting the reality of your situation, as opposed to the appearance of your situation.
- Taking action towards what you need, as opposed to what you want.
- Making a difficult choice between what you want and what you need.
- New equilibrium: What does it look like when you are returned home?

5) Notice how these four major story points are creating connective tissue. Be curious about how you get from one point to the next.

GROUP DISCUSSION TOPIC FOR TODAY

What is the truth that you're avoiding in your story? Can you share it with your group? Can you ask for support around it?

DAY 26

"We have all a better guide in ourselves, if we would attend to it, than any other person can be."

—JANE AUSTEN

DEFINE YOURSELF

Dear Writer,

Remember back a few weeks ago when I said that story involves the betrayal of a lie? And do you remember that experience of waking up, of realizing that you alone had the power to step out of the old paradigm, in spite of what everyone said? And you did it. And a gift appeared, whether in physical form at your doorstep or in the form of an insight.

The desire to write is really the desire to evolve, and evolution comes at a price. Freedom means letting go of our perceived security. In fact, you're going to discover through this process that your protagonist's *desire* actually prevents them from achieving their *goal*. It is only by letting go (which is different than giving up) that we can experience whether or not our desire belongs in our life.

Wisdom only arrives with the loss of innocence. Connection happens as the result of surrendering our ego. Intimacy occurs when we risk losing the one we love. Transformation demands that we say goodbye to something we cherished. This is not a bad thing, but simply a rite of passage. Lean into it. You can be stripped of your title, your castle, and even disowned. But is it worth the cost of your soul?

Don't sell yourself short. You know the truth — and it is that you are more courageous, resilient, and magnificent than anyone yet knows. Be willing to surrender the trappings of your former self, so that your transformed self can finally embrace you. Define yourself through your transformation, and don't allow anyone else to do it for you.

Until tomorrow,
Al

WRITING EXERCISES FOR TODAY

1) Write for five minutes on each of the following prompts, beginning with:

- It's been far too long since I . . .
- I feel intense loyalty towards . . .
- I know this isn't logical but . . .
- I feel misunderstood about . . .

2) With your nondominant hand, write an eight minute stream-of-consciousness dialogue, between you and your inner self, beginning with: "Tell me about a debt that you can never repay." Explore and listen and notice.

3) Write for twenty minutes, exploring in greater detail particular events from your life.

4) Explore these four structural elements from the third act (final section) of your story. Notice how all of these experiences are connected by the same primal desire.

- Accepting the reality of your situation, as opposed to the appearance of your situation.
- Taking action towards what you need, as opposed to what you want.

- Making a difficult choice between what you want and what you need.
- New equilibrium: What does it look like when you are returned home?

5) Notice how these four major story points are creating connective tissue. Be curious about how you get from one point to the next.

GROUP DISCUSSION TOPIC FOR TODAY

Do you see how your protagonist is beginning to understand their situation in a new way?

DAY 27

"All truth passes through three stages. First, it is ridiculed. Second, it is violently opposed. Third, it is accepted as self-evident."

—ARTHUR SCHOPENHAUER

YOUR STORY IS VALID

Dear Writer,

As you explore more deeply, are you hitting some raw nerves? Are you questioning whether or not you should be doing this? Are you questioning your own perception of reality? Do you see how the work of constructing a coherent narrative can throw you off and make you question everything, including your sanity?

For writers, sanity is overrated. Stay primal. Follow the scent. Your memoir is not a quest for logic, or an attempt to even a score. As storytellers, we are horrible mathematicians — the whole must always be greater than the sum of its parts. I grew up in a chronically academic home. Everything was charts and graphs, statistics and empirical evidence. The only problem with the facts is that if they are not viewed through an empathetic lens, there is no room for miracles. And we are witness to miracles every day. A drunk gets sober. A child forgives a parent. A woman leaves an abusive relationship. Siblings reunite.

Elliot Page's memoir, Pageboy, is a powerful account of his journey as a transgender guy. He explores the terror of coming out, first to himself, and then, as a public figure, to the rest of the world. He imagines that he could lose everything – or he could lose himself. One does not need to be trans to relate to the primal desire for authenticity, to stand in one's truth, consequences be damned. Elliot Page risks his private life, his career, his physical safety – and yet, the cost of remaining in the shadows of his true self is ultimately too great to bear.

Remember this: Your story is a miracle. Do you see the triumph of your spirit as it battles with reason and logic and ego? Do you see your bravery, your magnificence?

Remember this: Your story is valid. Trust it. Don't get thrown off the scent. In the end, your truth will prevail.

Until tomorrow,
Al

WRITING EXERCISES FOR TODAY

1) Write for five minutes on each of the following prompts, beginning with:

- The meanest thing anyone ever said to me was . . .
- I don't actually remember this, but I'm told that . . .
- I would describe myself as . . .
- The person who understands me best is . . .

2) With your nondominant hand, write an eight-minute stream-of-consciousness dialogue, between you and your inner self, beginning with: "Tell me the most intimate moment of your life." Explore and listen and notice.

3) Write for twenty minutes, exploring in greater detail particular events from your life.

4) Explore these four structural elements from the third act (final section) of your story. Notice how all of these experiences are con-

nected by the same primal desire.

- Accepting the reality of your situation, as opposed to the appearance of your situation.
- Taking action towards what you need, as opposed to what you want.
- Making a difficult choice between what you want and what you need.
- New equilibrium: What does it look like when you are returned home?

5) Notice how these four major story points are creating connective tissue. Be curious about how you get from one point to the next.

GROUP DISCUSSION TOPIC FOR TODAY

You begin writing your first draft in two days. How are you feeling about this? Is there something that you still need to know before you begin? Can you make space and trust that it will be revealed to you?

DAY 28

"Life is much too important to take seriously."
—OSCAR WILDE

HUMOR

Dear Writer,

Humor isn't punchlines; it is a point of view that sees the madness, the ridiculous, the absurdity of life. Your memoir has scope, and if your point of view doesn't include a certain sense of humor, you may not be seeing the larger picture.

Notice where humor lives in your story. While the events may be disturbing, even grim, without humor there may be no context for the pain.

There is nothing that you cannot write about, but give us the space to catch our breath, to gain objectivity, so that we are ready and willing to submit ourselves to the parts that require our hearts to break.

Until tomorrow,
Al

WRITING EXERCISES FOR TODAY

1) Write for five minutes on each of the following prompts, beginning with:

- The last time I drank too much I . . .
- The family member I am closest to is . . .
- Something that I wouldn't trade for the world is . . .
- A time I was too suspicious or cynical was . . .

2) With your nondominant hand, write an eight-minute stream-of-consciousness dialogue, between you and your inner self, beginning with: "Tell me about a time you were too trusting." Explore and listen and notice.

3) Write for twenty minutes, exploring in greater detail particular events from your life.

4) Explore these four structural elements from the third act (final section) of your story. Notice how all of these experiences are connected by the same primal desire.

- Accepting the reality of your situation, as opposed to the appearance of your situation.
- Taking action towards what you need, as opposed to what you want.
- Making a difficult choice between what you want and what you need.
- New equilibrium: What does it look like when you are returned home?

5) Notice how these four major story points are creating connective tissue. Be curious about how you get from one point to the next.

GROUP DISCUSSION TOPIC FOR TODAY

Did you have a breakthrough today? Can you trust that you don't need to have the whole story worked out in order to begin the first draft?

writing the first draft

WEEK 5

ACT ONE: THE BEGINNING

This week you begin writing the first draft of your memoir. You are going to spend the next three weeks writing Act One. This week you are going to write roughly a third of the way through your first act to the inciting incident. This is the time to turn off your internal editor and let it rip. Don't concern yourself with the quality of the prose. That comes later in the rewrite.

DAY 29

"A book must start somewhere. One brave letter must volunteer to go first, laying itself on the line in an act of faith, from which a word takes heart and follows, drawing a sentence into its wake. From there, a paragraph amasses, and soon a page, and the book is on its way, finding a voice, calling itself into being."

—**RUTH OZEKI**, *The Book of Form and Emptiness*

BEGINNING YOUR FIRST DRAFT

Dear Writer,

Starting today, you will spend the next nine weeks writing the first draft of your memoir. You're going to do this in a somewhat modular fashion, writing up to a different story point each week. Each story point is simply a key experience in your protagonist's journey.

Remember that story structure is not a formula. There are no rules. It is simply the DNA of your protagonist's transformation, and there are a series of experiences that your protagonist must go through to arrive at this transformed place. This does not mean that your story necessarily needs to be told in chronological order, but there does need to be a context for your opening.

INCITING INCIDENT

This week we are writing up to the inciting incident. Think in terms of what your reader needs to know in order for there to be a context for this incident. Remember, it is not what happens, but the meaning we ascribe to this event that provides context, or a "way in" for your reader. This is your "Why is this day unlike any other?" moment. This is the moment that sets your story into motion. Without this moment, there will be no context for what follows.

Here are some things to consider for your opening:

1. What is this thing about? Do you have an image or an idea for how you would like to dramatize or convey your theme? This is the overarching dramatic question or primal desire that carries your story to some sort of transformative moment. It is important to be thinking about this from the very beginning — however, at the same time, do not concern yourself with nailing your opening. Just start writing. If you give yourself permission to write poorly, and just get moving, you will eventually, and probably quite soon, hook into something that grabs your interest.

2. Remember that when it comes to a story point, it is not what happens, but the meaning we ascribe to what happens, that provides context for the event. Very quickly, write a list of everything that your reader needs to know or experience in order for your inciting incident to have its fullest impact.

3. Don't confuse the issue of your memoir with the theme. The issue is what it seems to be about (the plot), while the theme is the primal experience that is ultimately reframed through the story.

In Frank McCourt's memoir, *Angela's Ashes*, the issue is poverty while the theme is survival. In Jeanette Walls' memoir, *The Glass Castle*, the issue is also poverty, but the theme is more about self-sufficiency and adaptability. However, in both memoirs, the protagonist must betray a lie in order to free themselves from the bondage of their past.

Remember, you do not need to know exactly how your memoir ends, but it is helpful to have a sense of your protagonist's experience at the end. This will provide context for how far they've come from the beginning.

Until tomorrow,
Al

GROUP DISCUSSION TOPIC FOR TODAY
How are you feeling about beginning your first draft today?

WEEK 5: THOUGHTS AND REMINDERS

- Don't feel hemmed in by your outline. The outline is a document you create so you know what you're straying from.

- In the first draft, don't concern yourself with grammar, punctuation, or syntax. Just get the story down.

- Don't protect your characters.

- Write your first draft for yourself. Give yourself permission to never show it to anyone.

- Be willing to write the forbidden.

- Trust that your story won't look exactly like you thought it would. That's not a bad thing.

- Show, don't tell. Find ways to dramatize exposition by putting your characters into conflict and keeping them there.

- Let your story find its own pace.

- If it feels like your story is flatlining, inquire into your worthy antagonists. Notice the conflict or tension that arises.

- Write your first draft quickly, while allowing yourself to experience the beat-by-beat details of your story.
- Don't go back and rewrite anything. Keep moving forward.
- Make your memoir your top priority. Get it done first each day.

HOMEWORK FOR THE WEEK

1. Write a quick point-form outline from the beginning of your memoir to the inciting incident. (Twenty minutes maximum.)
2. This week, write up to the inciting incident in your memoir.

(There will be no more writing exercises. Your sole focus now is to complete your first draft.)

DAY 30

"Man's external form, marvelously constructed, is not much as compared with the divine soul that dwells inside that structure."

—LEONARDO DA VINCI

CONTEXT

Dear Writer,

Don't assume that your reader understands the context. We're only interested in what happens when we understand what it means to you. Have you ever had someone tell you a story and you still had no idea what they were talking about? Perhaps someone tells you, "I'm getting a divorce." What is your response? Well certainly it would depend on the context. It might be inappropriate to express your condolences if the person is beaming with joy. Depending on the situation, this news could mean anything — it could be devastating, comical, or absurd.

Without context, your reader is lost. As a storyteller you must be curious not only about the event you're relaying, but also in providing sufficient backstory or exposition to support the event.

The purpose of your memoir is to reveal a transformation. As you write your opening, you are holding a candle for your protagonist's transformation at the end of the story. In this way, you will stay connected to the reason you're telling the story. Your memoir is not a simple recounting of a series of events — it's a story that builds in meaning as it progresses, an examination of an internal struggle that is dramatized externally. You're tracking, in a compelling and truthful way, your journey to a new understanding.

Perhaps you're wondering if you're suitably transformed, if you're even qualified to write this story. Don't confuse transformation with some vague notion of enlightenment. Just because you still struggle does not mean that you are not qualified to write this story. We are spiritual beings having a human experience. Our struggle never fully ends. We will always battle our egos, question our motives, and second-guess our intentions. Ironically, when we take the risk of revealing our humanness, it provides a context for our exceptional strength and courage.

Until tomorrow,
Al

GROUP DISCUSSION TOPIC FOR TODAY

Were you surprised when your narrator began to speak to you? Are they funnier, more serious, more earnest, sadder or grumpier than you thought they would be? Are you trusting the voice?

DAY 31

"Without contraries is no progression. Attraction and repulsion, reason and energy, love and hate, are necessary to human existence."

—WILLIAM BLAKE

BOTH ARE TRUE

Dear Writer,

The transformation in your memoir is revealed by integrating two opposing forces. While your memoir begins with a dramatic question or thesis statement, its conclusion is not so much an empirical answer to that question but an integration or synthesis of the two opposing forces.

Here's a true story: I was terrified to get married. So scared in fact that I broke up with my fiancée in couples therapy. While I had proposed to Mary-Beth, I conveniently dodged setting a date.

When she insisted, we went to therapy and I patiently explained to the therapist, "Mary-Beth doesn't understand that I sometimes really hate her, and I don't think it's a good idea for me to be married."

Mary-Beth burst out laughing and said, "I think that's called love."

I didn't know how to be in a relationship. I only knew how to be alone. Isolation, while not exactly comfortable, was familiar, and it felt safe. I was afraid that when Mary-Beth saw the real me, she would run for the hills, and perhaps telling her that I sometimes hated her was an attempt to show her just how troubled I was. Ironically, with that stunning revelation on the table, I was safely ready to get married.

The truth is that while I thought I was afraid of commitment, I was really afraid of abandonment. I had never stayed in a relationship long enough to experience the exquisite terror of letting someone get to know me, and fearing what would happen as a result. Bolting from relationships is a necessary survival strategy when you don't believe that you're inherently lovable.

It wasn't until I committed that I began to investigate the possibility that I might actually be lovable — even writing this makes me feel queasy. In fact, while I was committing to Mary-Beth, I was really committing to walking through the discomfort of accepting that someone else loved me in spite of my imperfections. My "hatred" of Mary-Beth was really fear. How dare you love me!

Notice the contradictions in your story. Lean into them. Both are true.

Until tomorrow,
Al

GROUP DISCUSSION TOPIC FOR TODAY

How are you feeling about writing a messy first draft — not going back and rewriting, and just letting it rip?

DAY 32

"The most important things to remember about backstory are that (a) everyone has a history and (b) most of it isn't very interesting. Stick to the parts that are, and don't get carried away with the rest."
> —STEPHEN KING

BACKSTORY

Dear Writer,

The challenge in writing the beginning of your memoir is that you are doing multiple things simultaneously. You are establishing the world, introducing the characters, dramatizing the theme, and attempting to the move the story forward in some way so that you can hold your reader's interest.

All these things require finding creative ways to dramatize or disguise exposition. What you don't want to do is simply tell your reader what they need to know. Instead, identify your inciting incident — if it seems like you have multiple inciting incidents, then just pick one. And then, make a list of all the things that your reader needs to know or experience in order to provide context for this incident.

Once you have done that, you can let go of your notes and just allow the story to unfold. You don't need to manufacture ways to convey exposition. You will notice that your subconscious will naturally reach for these images and ideas in order to convey the exposition.

Until tomorrow,
Al

GROUP DISCUSSION TOPIC FOR TODAY

Do you have a sense of your first act structure? The inciting incident? Opposing argument? End of Act One decision?

DAY 33

*"Believing you are unworthy of love and belonging or
that who you are authentically is a sin or is wrong,
is deadly. Who you are is beautiful and amazing."*
—LAVERNE COX

THERE ARE NO UGLY TREES

Dear Writer,

People are always talking about how they need to be better, to improve themselves, to change, but I don't think that is correct. Think of yourself as a tree. Does a tree need to change? Does a pine tree need to turn into an oak tree to be acceptable? Of course not. Trees are perfect as they are. Trees, like people, don't actually change but they grow.

Every tree is unique, shaped by the elements; the thick cantilevered trunk of the weeping willow bent out over the rushing river, its roots gripping tightly to the banks, tells the story of seasons weathered and obstacles endured. Every tree was born perfect and rather alike, but due to age and circumstance, each becomes its own unique self, suffused, as Dylan Thomas would say, by "the force that through the green fuse drives the flower."

Building a story is often a counter-intuitive process. Our job, as writers, is not to try to improve or manipulate the circumstances of our characters in order to control the narrative, but often to shed our defenses, our masks, our pretenses, in order to allow the story to become what it was meant to be.

Notice in your story where your characters' struggles inevitably move you in the direction of confronting some unpleasant aspect of yourself, something that you may have been hoping to avoid. Your job as a storyteller is not to finesse or deny this moment, but to be willing to shed a delusion, a fear, a limiting belief that you may have about yourself or the world. Notice the quiet dread or even anguish this elicits — it might feel like you're crawling out of your skin.

Notice in nature how trees shed their leaves, how animals shed their fur. Well, emotionally and psychologically, we are doing this as well. Creating a story is an evolutionary process, which is less about adding, and more about letting go.

Your goal as an artist is not to become more acceptable to others, but to go deeper into who you truly are — to be authentic. But this isn't safe. There will be antagonism, especially in the beginning. The universe will test you to make sure you are sincere. No one gives you permission to take up space, to shout your truth. You must claim it for yourself.

But you have allies, a support system. You have people who believe in you, even when you don't believe in yourself. You can depend on these people, and you are someone others can depend upon as well. Your strength lies in your vulnerability.

Things have been said. Things have been done. You have internalized them in spite of your attempts to do otherwise. Perhaps you have even done things that you are ashamed of, things that you regret. This doesn't make you bad or unworthy. It makes you human.

Sometimes you might hold onto guilt with the belief that it makes you a better person. You may even believe that if you forgive yourself for the mistakes of your past and truly let it go, you are somehow betraying the ones you've harmed.

If you don't let go, or at least examine the burden of self-recrimination, you are limiting the potential of your story to affect others. Without self-forgiveness, there will be no transformation. If you could have done it any other way, you likely would have, and just like the tree that has weathered the elements, your survival strategies mark and shape your being. Amidst all of the challenges and setbacks, what you have to express is true and beautiful and valid. After all, there are no ugly trees.

Until tomorrow,
Al

GROUP DISCUSSION TOPIC FOR TODAY

Are you allowing yourself to be surprised by the process? Remember, you're not the "author," you're the "channel." Take the risk of allowing yourself to be surprised.

DAY 34

"The smiles of the unhappiest are often the widest."
—MOKOKOMA MOKHONOANA

TAKING OFF THE MASK

Dear Writer,

A common dilemma in addiction memoir's is the double life. In Jerry Stahl's darkly funny and emotionally unsettling memoir of alienation and despair, *Permanent Midnight* tells the story of his hustle to maintain a semblance of normalcy as a network television writer struggling to keep his increasingly out of control drug habit a secret while losing jobs, relationships and nearly his life as he strategizes on how to get his next fix. In Mathew Perry's memoir, *Friends, Lovers and the Big Terrible Thing*, he tells the tale of his struggle to navigate a successful acting career while privately spiraling out of control in a decade's long battle with alcoholism and opiate addiction.

While the double life is a common theme in addiction memoirs, if you scratch the surface of most memoirs, you'll see that on some level the protagonist has a secret — that there's a disconnect or a dissonance between their external and internal world.

Do you see where this experience may live in your memoir? Do you see where you're keeping secrets from others, or even from yourself? What are you not admitting to yourself? Where in the story are you allowing yourself to be taken advantage of, or perhaps you are the one taking advantage? Notice where you might be unwilling to speak your truth, to stand up for yourself, or to let go of some form of vice? Nobody is all good or all bad, but the journey of memoir often involves the integration of one's public and private selves by relinquishing their mask.

Notice where your protagonist is withholding the truth from themselves or others. Notice where this impulse may live in the opening of your story, so that there is a context for how this impulse is shed by the end.

Until tomorrow,
Al

GROUP DISCUSSION TOPIC FOR TODAY

Is the universe throwing you any curveballs? Are you able to stay committed to your story?

DAY 35

"A memoir forces me to stop and remember careful-
ly. It is an exercise in truth. In a memoir, I look at
myself, my life, and the people I love the most in the
mirror of the blank screen. In a memoir, feelings are
more important than facts, and to write honestly, I
have to confront my demons."

—ISABEL ALLENDE

CONFRONTING YOUR DEMONS

Dear Writer,

We are forever running toward and away from our heart's desire. This is the nature of dilemma, and our lives are filled with them. We want adventure, but we also want security. We want connection, but we also want freedom. We want purpose, but we want to play and have fun. We want immortality, but we don't want to age. We want to be special, but we don't want to lose our sense of belonging.

Have you ever watched a small child running away from their mother? They want to be free, but the moment they see something unfamiliar, they race back to the security of mom. Notice how the desire to be free has no context without the need to feel safe. It is our connection to this core dilemma that keeps our narrative anchored to the truth, and allows it to build in meaning as it progresses.

In Temple Grandin's memoir, Thinking in Pictures, she explores her struggle with feeling marginalized as an autistic person, but what makes this book a seminal work is that, while not mini-mizing the challenges of an autistic person, it celebrates the excep-tional strengths and special gifts of autistic people. What makes the memoir universal is that, at its core, it is an examination of how we all have our own special qualities, and how easy it is to compare our weaknesses to others, rather than celebrating our unique gifts.

If you're feeling confused, or that a scene isn't quite doing what you want it to be doing, just gently return to the core primal desire that is driving you. Notice the dilemma at the heart of this desire. You will inevitably discover that your demon is borne out of the false belief you make out of this desire.

Remember, it is not your job to make this demon go away. In-stead, make friends with it. Acknowledge it. And then gently but firmly, let it know that you are now in charge.

Now, go ahead and write the scene that your demon told you not to write.

Until tomorrow,
Al

GROUP DISCUSSION TOPIC FOR TODAY
Is your protagonist actively pursuing their goal? If the scene feels flat, ask yourself, "What is my protagonist *doing* to get what they want?»

WEEK 6

ACT ONE:
THE OPPOSING ARGUMENT

This week you are writing up to the opposing argument, which is approximately two-thirds of the way through your first act. The opposing argument is where your reader begins to understand that what appeared to be a problem is, in fact, a dilemma.

DAY 36

*"The dilemma is that if one does not risk anything
one risks even more."*   —ERICA JONG

OPPOSING ARGUMENT

Dear Writer,

This week you are writing up to the opposing argument. This is
where there is some kind of antagonistic response to your protagonist's desire. This is where the stakes rise and you begin to see that
you struggling not with a problem, but with a dilemma. Your goal
with the opposing argument is to find a way to dramatize this experience for your reader. It is not enough to explain that you have a
dilemma. We want to see how it plays out in your life.

Notice how the stakes are rising from the very beginning of
your story. Notice how the inciting incident dramatizes your dramatic question, while the opposing argument amplifies it.

For example, in *Romeo and Juliet*, the story begins with Romeo
heartbroken because his relationship has ended with Rosalind. He
wants true love, but he questions whether or not it exists. The dramatic question is "Does true love exist?"

And then, at the inciting incident, he sees Juliet through the
window. Do you see that without the dramatic question of "Does
true love exist?" there is no context for what it means when he sees
Juliet?

Notice also, that there cannot be an opposing argument without there first being an inciting incident. Once Romeo sees Juliet

through the window, he enters the party and dances with her . . . and then, Juliet's cousin Tybalt discovers this interloper, who happens to be the enemy of Juliet's family, and he threatens to kill him. This is the opposing argument, the antagonistic response to your protagonist. Now Romeo has a dilemma. He may have found true love. Is it worth risking his life?

And of course this leads to his decision at the end of the first act. This is where he makes a decision to proclaim his love by entering into enemy territory to stand under her balcony.

Notice the elegance of these four Act One story points, and how they each move the story forward:

- Theme/dramatic question: Does true love exist?
- Inciting Incident: Romeo sees Juliet through the window.
- Opposing argument: Romeo's love for Juliet could get him killed.
- Decision at end of act one: Romeo decides to proclaim his love in spite of the consequences.

Lastly, the opposing argument is often one of the foggiest story points. It is sometimes only after completing your first draft that it becomes apparent. It is less important to nail this story point than it is to explore it. You do not need to have a clear sense of your protagonist's opposing argument in order to continue writing.

Until tomorrow,
Al

GROUP DISCUSSION TOPIC FOR TODAY

Are you noticing a difference between where you thought your story would go, or what you thought it might "feel" like, and how it is actually revealing itself? Do you find yourself judging this, or simply remaining curious and charging forward?

WEEK 6: THOUGHTS AND REMINDERS

- Remember, you cannot make a mistake. Surprise yourself. Be willing to write the forbidden. While you know the facts of your story, you are beginning to glimpse deeper truths.

- If your writing feels stale, be curious about what you're trying to protect. Is there a fear that you are unwilling to reveal? Be curious about your antagonists. Remember, we love to the extent that we hate.

- What does our protagonist's unresolved state look like? Are you willing to write from that raw, vulnerable place?

- If you are not connected to the tension, you should stop writing, take a breath, and be curious about the specific conflict between your protagonist and antagonist. Put them into action. The stakes are life and death.

- Our subconscious performs miracles on demand. It is not our job to figure out how to get to the end. Our job is to have a "sense" of the ending. Is it a story of courage, love, hope, redemption, revenge, or is it a cautionary tale?

CHECKLIST OF QUESTIONS

1. Is your protagonist active? What are they doing to get what they want?

2. Are we meeting your main characters early on?

3. Do we understand the dilemma at the heart of your story?

4. Do we care about your protagonist? What makes us care? A powerful desire!

5. Do you have a clear inciting incident? Without this, we won't know why you are telling us this story.

6. If your story begins with a lot of backstory, be curious about the present urgency for your protagonist.

7. Don't be married to your outline. Trust the aliveness of your characters.

HOMEWORK FOR THE WEEK

1. Write a quick point-form outline from the inciting incident up to the opposing argument. (Twenty minutes maximum.)

2. Write up to your opposing argument this week.

DAY 37

*"It is good to have an end to journey towards; but it
is the journey that matters, in the end."*
—URSULA K. LE GUIN

RESISTANCE

Dear Writer,

Are you feeling resistance to writing? Resistance often rears its head when you are on the verge of a breakthrough. This is because as much as you would like your situation to improve, you don't particularly like change, even positive change. It is unfamiliar, and you are forced to adapt.

Are you feeling bored by your writing? Fear often masquerades as boredom. Perhaps you're thinking, "Who cares? Will anyone read this? Does it matter? Perhaps I'd be better off spending my time doing something else." Sometimes, out of fear, you choose to give up in the same way that an animal rolls over and plays dead when it is in danger of a predator.

You must be aware of this. You must expect this and counter act it. While writing may appear to look like a polite way to spend the afternoon, writing memoir involves claiming your truth, and this often brings with it an opposing argument.

You are a pioneer. Your truth matters, even if your inner voice is shaky, and you're not quite sure where the narrative is taking you. Deep within you lies your inner warrior. It is not interested in the result. It understands that your liberation lies in the daily process of putting your truth on the page, in spite of what the voices in your head are saying.

Until tomorrow,
Al

GROUP DISCUSSION TOPIC FOR TODAY

Story is a sensory experience. Are you employing the five senses? What does rain smell like? What does silence sound like? What does grief taste like?

DAY 38

"Thought is subversive and revolutionary, destructive and terrible. Thought is merciless to privilege, established institutions, and comfortable habits.... Thought is great and swift and free."
—BERTRAND RUSSELL

BE SUBVERSIVE

Dear Writer,

I believe that, by definition, making art is a subversive act. Nobody ever gives you permission to challenge their perception of reality, and yet, when you do, they may thank you later.

Notice in your memoir how you are challenging the status quo. Your memoir begins with a dramatic question, and through your story the argument gets played out between accepting the current state of things, or making a decision to see things in a new way.

Embrace this aspect of your story. Make peace with the fact that you are betraying a lie. Give yourself permission to be dangerous on the page, and acknowledge that, on some level, you are upending a long-held belief. Give yourself permission to be in the unknown for a while. Does it feel uncomfortable? Scary? Unsettling? You know something that no one else knows. This notion might seem crazy, but it is true. Take a breath and give yourself permission to tell it. Sometimes it feels like we're going crazy when we're actually going sane.

Until tomorrow,
Al

GROUP DISCUSSION TOPIC FOR TODAY

As you write your first act, are you beginning to see your ending differently? Are you surprising yourself? Are you beginning to have revelations on where your story needs to go? And are you willing to hold your story loosely enough to allow for these intuitive impulses to guide you? Remember, everything you write either belongs or is leading you to what ultimately belongs in your story. You cannot make a mistake in this process.

DAY 39

"You have been criticizing yourself for years and it hasn't worked. Try approving of yourself and see what happens."   **—Louise L. Hay**

WHERE'S THE LOVE?

Dear Writer,

In every story, love is the mystery that is always on the table. I don't mean romantic love, or familial love, but self-love. In story, love is not a noun, but a verb. It is an action you take that allows your heart to open and moves you in the direction of greater inner freedom. Your reader experiences self-love through your protagonist's actions, particularly in the third act.

Regardless of the tone of your memoir, when you connect to the love, you connect to your protagonist's difficult choice at the climax — the choice between the old way and the new way. Your protagonist often sets out on a quest to change the world "out there" only to discover that what needed changing was the world "within." Self-love sounds like it should be simple to achieve, but it isn't. It often involves a betrayal.

Notice in your story where your protagonist is withholding in some way, perhaps not speaking their truth. Notice the fear, the resistance to living in an authentic way. We tend to see the world through the lens of our past experience, rather than the reality of our present circumstance. Self-love is a willingness to shed what isn't working, in spite of the apparent security it provides.

There may also be a point where you're confronted with your protagonist's limitations, and you may question how you can ever be worthy of self-love. Don't confuse your protagonist's actions with their true identity. You may think that what your protagonist has done is irredeemable, but redemption comes from within. When you approach your protagonist's struggle as a problem, you may get stuck, but when you see that they're struggling with a dilemma, your imagination unlocks new possibilities. Your memoir is an invitation to let go of a limiting belief that you have about yourself or the world. Notice how your protagonist's strategy to get what they want is also their flaw. Self-love comes from letting go of the idea that your salvation comes from an external source.

Until tomorrow,
Al

GROUP DISCUSSION TOPIC FOR TODAY

Does the scene feel flat? If you know you're going to go left in a scene, then you must go right. Meaning gets conveyed through tension or conflict. Allow yourself to explore moving in the opposite direction of where you think your characters would go. This will help to amplify their dilemma.

DAY 40

"Get it down. Take chances. It may be bad, but that's
the only way you can do anything really good."
—**WILLIAM FAULKNER**

PERMISSION TO WRITE POORLY

Dear Writer,

You must give yourself permission to write poorly in your first
draft. Do not pay attention to the quality of your prose. Do not
concern yourself with grammar, punctuation, or syntax. When we
attempt to write the polish before we write the first draft, we tend
to get stuck.

Allow your focus to be on telling the story. Allow yourself to be
surprised by all of the interesting ideas and scenarios that emerge.
Don't worry about the language.

And please, do not go back and rewrite or edit. This is why
writing longhand can be helpful, especially if you are a perfection-
ist. Just keep marching forwards.

Until tomorrow,
Al

GROUP DISCUSSION TOPIC FOR TODAY

Where's the love? In every story, love is the mystery that is always
on the table. Even in the most contentious relationships, notice
where the love is.

DAY 41

"The sole meaning of life is to serve humanity."
—LEO TOLSTOY

MEANING

Dear Writer,

Memoir is a search for meaning. When you recount the argument you had with your spouse about how you wanted a kid but they didn't, be curious about *why* you're telling us this. What is the argument really about? What is it that you want? What does having a kid represent? Be curious. Does it represent security, identity, validation, purpose, power, fulfillment? Always be asking yourself, "What am I trying to express through this event?" And then be on the lookout for patterns. Notice how the search never changes. We never stop looking for connection, or validation, or success, we merely reframe our relationship to these things.

Plot is "what happens." Theme is "what it means." Your goal as a storyteller is to marry plot to theme. It is not enough to tell us what happens if it is not anchored to meaning.

Have you ever been cornered at a party by someone who started rambling on about some event from their life, and you found yourself wondering, "Why are you telling me this?"

It's the same with memoir. You must stay connected to why you're telling the story. The "why" is the dramatic question that is found in your protagonist's dilemma. This "why" becomes the through line of your story.

The through line often presents itself as a sort of "feeling tone" — a desire for clarity, a craving for an answer that never quite seems to arrive, a quiet yearning for resolution.

Notice how the meaning that you make out of your theme gets reframed through your story. In the beginning, the desire may be self-serving, but by the end the purpose is not ego-driven — it's in service to a larger purpose.

Examples of reframing themes:

BEGINNING
- I'll be free when I escape.
- I'll have justice when they suffer.
- The truth lies in the facts.

ENDING
- I'll be free when I take responsibility.
- Justice means compassion.
- The truth is how I interpret the facts.

Notice how we must experience your protagonist's struggle in the first act in order to experience the transformation in Act Three.

Until tomorrow,
Al

GROUP DISCUSSION TOPIC FOR TODAY

Narrative drive — Are you staying connected to what your protagonist wants? Is it primal?

DAY 42

*"Good judgment comes from experience, and
experience comes from bad judgment."*
—RITA MAE BROWN

EXPERIENCE

Dear Writer,

Experience conveys meaning.

Your job as a storyteller is to track your characters' experiences in a compelling and believable way that leads to a transformation. But don't confuse experience with feelings. Feelings don't mean much. They're like the weather channel, forever changing. If you tell your reader that you felt sad, they want to know why. Your experience is the "Why?" If you succeed in telling us why you felt sad, you will likely discover that you don't need to tell us how you felt.

This is why plot without experience is useless. If you simply tell us what happened, your reader will be confused. We must be in the characters' experience in order for meaning to be conveyed.

A writer once asked me to explain what I meant by "experience conveys meaning," and so, I made up a story that has a plot but no experience to guide you to its meaning. Here it is:

Betty comes home and tells Tom she wants to end their twenty-year marriage. Tom quits his job and flies to Paris. He takes a taxi out to a carrot farm in Normandy, and when the cab pulls up, the carrot farmer runs out and embraces him. The two men weep together, and later that week they open a carrot juice stand at the end of the laneway called *Carrot Juice Charlie's*. Every Friday, they fire rockets into the night sky.

Okay. Are you bewildered? Good. You should be. While I've told you the plot, describing exactly what happened, it is bereft of experience, and remember, experience conveys meaning. Notice that every sentence you write must, in some way, be answering the question your ideal reader is asking: Why?

So, here's the story again, but now, each event will answer the question "Why?"

Betty comes home and tells Tom she wants a divorce. "After twenty years of marriage, you're still a stranger to me," she says. "I can't take it anymore."

Tom is blindsided by this news. Something shakes him awake, and he realizes that he must make a radical change in his life. He quits his job and flies to France, which is the last place he saw his father alive when he was a young boy.

He takes a taxi out to a carrot farm in Normandy, the place where his father fell dead from a heart attack while they were picking carrots together.

The farmer, Marcel, a dear friend of Tom's father rushes out of his house and embraces Tom. Marcel has been haunted for years by his inability to resuscitate Tom's dad, and his unending guilt at Tom becoming orphaned has led him to a life of drink. But something happens with Tom's appearance. Call it grace, but he senses a second chance at life.

Together Tom and Marcel decide to open a carrot juice stand at the end of the laneway. They call it *Carrot Juice Charlie's*, in honor of their beloved friend and father, and every Friday night they fire rockets into the sky.

Okay, it's a ridiculous story, but did you experience something? Do you see the difference between simply telling us what happened and imbuing it with meaning?

Take us into your characters' experiences and your story will build in meaning as it progresses.

Until tomorrow,
Al

GROUP DISCUSSION TOPIC FOR TODAY

Do you see how all your characters want the same thing at their core? What is it? Connection? Power? Meaning? Purpose? Control? Notice how it is this *uniformity of desire* that ironically creates the conflict in your story.

WEEK 7

ACT ONE:
YOUR PROTAGONIST MAKES A DECISION

Your goal for this week is to reach the end of Act One; the moment your protagonist makes a decision that they can't go back on. Notice the reluctance around this decision. This reluctance keeps us connected to your protagonist's dilemma, which is the throughline of your story.

DAY 43

"Once you make a decision, the universe conspires to make it happen."   —RALPH WALDO EMERSON

DECISION

Dear Writer,

This week you are writing up to the decision that your protagonist makes at the end of the first act. Notice how there is reluctance around this decision. Without a certain amount of reluctance there will be no tension, and without tension there is no meaning conveyed. Your protagonist's reluctance is what keeps the reader connected to your dilemma.

But don't confuse reluctance with indifference. While the decision you make is toward getting what you want, the reluctance is due to a certain misgiving, a "catch" of some sort.

When Romeo Montague discovers that Juliet belongs to the House of Capulet, he hesitates. While he desperately wants to proclaim his love, he fears that if he does then her father will kill him.

If Romeo merely saw Juliet through the window andinstantly professed his love to her without our knowing that their families are mortal enemies, there would be no tension. Hence, no story.

When Romeo makes that choice, the story builds in meaning, because we are experiencing the tension between his desire to be with his true love, coupled with his fear that this love could prove fatal.

Notice where your protagonist's desire leads to a decision that they cannot go back on. And notice where reluctance lives in this decision.

Until tomorrow,
Al

GROUP DISCUSSION TOPIC FOR TODAY

Have you made a list of what needs to happen to get from your protagonist's opposing argument to the end of their Act One decision?

WEEK 7: THOUGHTS AND REMINDERS

- You're not doing this alone. When you commit to a creative endeavor, you're tuning into a channel and all sorts of coincidences may happen to support you in completing your work.

- In order to complete your work, you may experience a shift in priorities. Sometimes your friends and family don't take kindly to this. This doesn't mean you're selfish. It just means the garbage might have to wait till tomorrow.

- You may notice that we have become a filter for our story and our daily lives. The people we hear and see, our environment, everything informs our work, giving us insights and ideas.

- "I'm not writing, but I'm thinking." Some days you don't put as many words down on the page. That's okay. Sometimes writing is pondering.

- Be curious about the metaphors in your story. Metaphors illuminate your story's deeper meaning.

- If a scene or an idea comes to you, write it down. If your characters seem to be taking on a life of their own, be curious about how you can support their choices.

- Be curious about a moment of reluctance that precedes your protagonist's decision at the end of Act One. Humans don't typically like change. We only change when we have run out of choices.

CHECKLIST OF QUESTIONS

1. Have I introduced the major characters in my story?

2. Do I understand their relationships to each other as functions of the story?

3. What is my protagonist's dilemma?

4. Do I have worthy antagonists?

5. Is the story moving through action? Am I showing rather than telling?

6. Do I have a sense of the decision my protagonist makes at the end of Act One?

7. Am I being specific?

8. Do I feel engaged with the tension or am I just logging words on the page?

9. Do I feel connected to what I want to express?

HOMEWORK FOR THE WEEK

1. Write a quick point-form outline from the opposing argument up to your protagonist's decision at the end of Act One. (Twenty minutes maximum.)

2. Write to the end of Act One.

DAY 44

"Growth demands a temporary surrender of security."   —GAIL SHEEHY

LET GO OF THE RESULT

Dear Writer,

When you let go of the result, you invite yourself to go to places that you might have never otherwise explored. If you must arrive safely then these places are too dangerous, too forbidden, and too treacherous to explore. But if you make the journey more important than the destination, and possess a curiosity greater than your fear, you will inevitably start to have insights and breakthroughs.

Stay in the process — this is where the thrill of creation lives. Dive into those places where you fear you will be misunderstood, disliked, judged, and even banished. If we do not see you struggle, make mistakes, and even cause harm, there will be no context for your liberation.

Until tomorrow,
Al

GROUP DISCUSSION TOPIC FOR TODAY

Do you have a sense of your protagonist's decision at the end of the first act? Do you see the reluctance around this decision? Do you see how this reluctance keeps us connected to your protagonist's dilemma?

DAY 45

*"Sometimes people surprise us. People we believe we
know."*   **—JOYCE CAROL OATES**

DON'T INDICATE

Dear Writer,

Have you ever watched a play performed in a community theater?
Let's face it, not every actor is Meryl Streep. Sometimes the per-
former "indicates" — they play sad by pouting, or angry by flaring
their nostrils, or mortified by balling their fists and grabbing their
cheeks; rather than allowing themselves to simply have an authentic experience, they try to do "more."
Don't do more. Your truth is more than enough.

Because the truth is that even when we're angry, we're not just
angry, we're probably also hurt, or scared, or maybe jealous or
guilty, and maybe even also horny or embarrassed. In other words,
it is rare to have one single pure emotion at a time. They are often
in conflict with other thoughts and feelings simultaneously.

As memoirists, we are prone to indicating, but we do it by trying to analyze our experience so that we can "portray it properly."
We can get so hung up on trying to do it right that we try to throw
a lasso around our experience — we try to tame it by naming it. But
when we name it, we kill it, because we're moving away from the
truth of it, the danger of it, the aliveness of it.

Let it be wild. Let it be nameless for a minute. Sit with the thrilling possibility that you will never get your heart's desire. Don't
panic. Don't go numb. Just sit for one minute. Seriously, set a timer.

I'm not kidding. Set a timer.

Notice how the sky didn't fall. Notice how thrilling and wondrous life is, even without your heart's desire. In fact, notice how your heart's desire might actually be preventing you from getting your soul's desire. This doesn't mean that you ought to quit pursuing your heart's desire, but what if you reframed it? What if you put your soul's desire ahead of it for a minute? What if you allowed your heart to truly break? What if it didn't matter that anyone ever read your memoir? What if you wrote it because the truth — your honest and sincere exploration — was enough? What if you allowed yourself to breathe for a minute, without breathlessly wishing that things were otherwise. Notice where this experience lives in your story.

You are the wise one on the hill, and when you write from this perspective, you will discover that you are able to contain the mystery of what it means to be you. Sit with the grief of your regret, without shaming yourself for it — this is just another way of going numb. Sit with the love you have for that inner child who tried their best, but something didn't go the way you planned it. Sit with your experience without shellacking it. Sit quietly with your breath, with the danger in your story, and just for a moment glimpse the possibility that your story can be filled with contradictions, and that, ironically, these contradictions are what makes your story universal. Ultimately, what connects us all is our broken heart. This is not victimhood, it is humanity.

Until tomorrow,
Al

GROUP DISCUSSION TOPIC FOR TODAY

Writing your first draft is like running a marathon. Are you getting enough rest? Are you creating down time so that you can recharge?

DAY 46

"May your choices reflect your hopes, not your fears."
—Nelson Mandela

YOU ARE UNIQUELY QUALIFIED

Dear Writer,

Look at what you've accomplished in six weeks! You've done a deep dive into the events from your life and you've begun to glimpse a narrative that leads to some kind of transformative experience.

This is a tremendous achievement.

If you are thinking that you should have the story all figured out, or that you don't quite know what your protagonist's dilemma is, that is okay. Remember that your dilemma is an experience, and therefore not something that is easy to quantify. Problems are solved, while dilemmas are resolved through a shift in perception. It is more important to ask the question than it is to answer it.

It seems it should go without saying that you are uniquely qualified to write your memoir. And yet, the voices lurk at the edges of your consciousness: Who do you think you are? Are you just a fraud? A wannabe? We live in a culture that mistakes logic for wisdom and fact for truth.

When I met with the publishers of my first novel (who had just paid me an obscene amount of money) I was flown to New York and took the elevator to the top of a skyscraper up to a room where seven publishing executives sat, and I was asked where I had studied creative writing. Was it Iowa Writers' workshop, or Irvine Writing Program? I hesitated before responding sheepishly that I didn't really study anywhere, at least not formally, and that frankly I just read a lot and wrote volumes in my bedroom for over a decade. Well, the room fell so quiet you could hear a cow fart in Saskatchewan. Imagine their dismay that their precious advance had been squandered on some unschooled Philistine.

I don't think it is essential that we endure a Darwinian vetting process to be given permission to write our truth. Whether conscious or not, our culture throws up all sorts of intellectual firewalls to dissuade or silence us.

There is a disparity of middle-aged white male privileged writers whose stories lead to an imbalance, a perception that these books reflect our collective reality. While the gap is narrowing, the disparity is real. Whenever I listen to discussions of literature on the radio, we seem expected to bring our sophisticated minds rather than our wild animal selves, our emotional curiosity, our spiritual hunger. We are expected to worship at the shrine of consensus, but one's truth is almost by definition subversive.

The irony is that what the marketplace is looking for is you. Your true voice. You must let go of your desire to appeal to some godlike patriarchy, some gatekeeper staring down their spectacles at you. You hold all the power. The emperor has no clothes.

Keep going.

Until tomorrow,
Al

GROUP DISCUSSION TOPIC FOR TODAY

Living your life as an artist (which is what you are) is an act of self-love. Our culture doesn't always support the notion of creative play (mild understatement.) If you are to thrive as an artist, it is helpful to consider what you truly value, otherwise you may spend years or even decades chasing after goals that were never yours to begin with.

DAY 47

"There is a world of difference between truth and facts. Facts can obscure the truth."
—MAYA ANGELOU

FACTS VERSUS TRUTH

Dear Writer,

I grew up in an academic family. Everything was statistics — "evidence-based." The problem is that the term "evidence" suggests a forgone conclusion, but the facts do not equal the truth, in fact, the two are often in opposition to each other.

It is not the evidence itself, but our interpretation of the evidence that matters, because let's face it, everyone has a bias. And how does one quantify the power of love, or forgiveness, or compassion? Not everything can be tested. Your goal in memoir is not simply to relate the facts, but to show us how the whole is greater than the sum of those facts.

Yes, the facts are important, but it is the interpretation of the facts that move your story beyond a polemic to a transformative experience. They did a psychological study years ago where they interviewed witnesses of a car accident to discover what happened and who was at fault. While everybody witnessed the same accident — the facts were identical — their interpretation of those facts varied widely.

In Javier Zamora's memoir, *Solito*, he recounts his journey as a nine-year old boy from El Salvador to the United States to be reunited with his parents. It is a treacherous and at times harrowing weekslong journey. While the boy's desire to be reunited is a fact, the story examines the question of whether or not he should make the trip. Is it worth it to risk one's life? The fact is that while this journey might be, statistically, a poor choice, the alternative is not an option.

Notice where the truth of your story lies beyond the facts, because what makes us care is that, in one way or another, your story is about the triumph of the human spirit.

Everybody's interpretation of the facts will vary, therefore, while your goal with memoir is to always present your experience as accurately as possible, remember that the facts are always in service to the larger truth.

Until tomorrow,
Al

GROUP DISCUSSION TOPIC FOR TODAY

Failure — What does this word mean to you? Does it elicit shame? Do you recoil at the sound, like you've just touched a hot stove? Or is it something to learn from, even celebrate? Is it an inevitable part of the creative process, an opportunity to course correct, to deepen your process? Is it the road to true wisdom?

DAY 48

"The most difficult thing is the decision to act. The rest is merely tenacity."   —Amelia Earhart

DECISIONS, DECISIONS

Dear Writer,

We are always making decisions. The decision at the end of your first act has a special flavor to it. It is a decision that moves you out of your ordinary world and into a new realm — and this decision often involves a certain amount of reluctance. It is often a sobering moment, because you are aware of the gravity of this choice.

The reluctance around the decision is what keeps your reader anchored to what the decision means — namely the cost, that you could fail, and that your failure carries some dire consequence. Don't confuse reluctance with indifference. There can be tremendous excitement surrounding the decision. The reluctance is connected to your trepidation of the potential downside.

Here are some examples of decisions that one cannot go back on:

- Telling a secret
- Proclaiming your love
- Accepting a proposal
- Accepting a promotion
- Revealing a truth
- Beginning an affair

- Taking responsibility
- Leaving home
- Standing up to authority
- Refusing to rescue a suffering loved one.

Notice how all of these decisions are attempts to get what you want. They all tap into that primal desire . . . and yet, notice how there is a certain reluctance attached to each of these decisions because of the dilemma. Let's look at some possible examples of reluctance based on these ten decisions:

- What if you don't keep my secret? Will you betray me?
- What if you don't love me back? Am I safe?
- What if I am committing to the wrong person? Am I committing out of security or love?
- I want the promotion, but now my former co-workers are my underlings. Am I giving up connection to my friends?
- Will this truth bring us together or tear us apart?
- Is this affair an escape or am I moving toward true love?
- Is this responsibility going to ruin my life or set me free?
- Is leaving home a mistake? Can I make it on my own?
- Am I sabotaging myself, or being true to myself?
- Am I responsible? And if I lose them, will I survive the guilt?

Notice the decision that your protagonist makes at the end of the first act, and also the reluctance surrounding this action.

Until tomorrow,
Al

GROUP DISCUSSION TOPIC FOR TODAY

What is your most recent breakthrough? Is your relationship to your creative breakthroughs shifting? Are you beginning to see that you are merely a channel, that you are cocreating this story with some deeper force, and that these breakthroughs are actually something you can begin to trust?

DAY 49

"That element of surprise is what I look for when I am writing. It is my way of judging what I am doing — which is never an easy thing to do."

—V.S. NAIPAUL

THE ELEMENT OF SURPRISE

Dear Writer,

The element of surprise exists not just at the level of a major plot twist, but also throughout the narrative in smaller and seemingly innocuous ways. The dilemma you face as a memoirist, is that you already know what is going to happen, while your characters have no idea. They don't know where the story is going, or even that they're in one. But story is not about what happens, it is about the meaning we ascribe to what happens.

Here's something to consider. If you know that a character in a scene is going left, you must explore the possibility of them going right. This means that as human beings we are always weighing our options. We rarely tumble blindly forward without due consideration.

In A.M. Holmes memoir, *The Mistress's Daughter*, the story begins with a letter from the author's birth mother (the author was adopted at birth), reaching out and requesting contact. While A.M. Holmes had been curious about her birth parents all her life, she had never sought them out. Is she curious to meet her birth mother? Yes. Does she fire a letter right back to her and schedule a meeting? No.

First, she processes her thoughts and feelings, and thus, creates a compelling narrative for the richly complex experience of having had your most major life decision made for you without your permission. In fact, she seriously considers not responding, thus creating a sense of surprise when she ultimately does reach out. By employing the element of surprise, meaning is conveyed.

If the story had moved directly from the author's receipt of the letter to the meeting with her mother, which is essentially what happened, at least externally, the story would have been stripped of meaning, because while the plot involves a reunification of the author to her birth parents, that is merely a backdrop for Holmes to explore the theme of identity that led her to a deeper understanding of her place in the world.

Until tomorrow,
Al

GROUP DISCUSSION TOPIC FOR TODAY

Is it scary to trust the process? Does it feel unfamiliar to truly relax and know that you have given birth to characters that are taking on a life of their own?

WEEK 8

ACT TWO: YOUR PROTAGONIST EXPERIENCES FALSE HOPE

This week you are writing up to the moment where your protagonist experiences *false hope*. As a result of your protagonist's decision at the end of Act One, they set out on a journey towards achieving their goal. This first step on the journey offers the tantalizing hope that success is within their grasp. This moment is essential in their journey, as it will provide context for what must be surrendered by the end of Act Two.

DAY 50

"Hunger makes a thief of any man."
—**PEARL S. BUCK**

FALSE HOPE AND YEARNING

Dear Writer,

Once your protagonist makes a decision that they can't go back on, they set out on a journey toward achieving their goal. As they proceed, there is often a moment early in this quest where it appears that what they seek is within their grasp. This is often a private moment of success for your protagonist, a sort of "Yes, I'm going to win," type of moment.

Can you recognize where this experience might live for your protagonist? Let's say you made a decision to marry someone because you believed that it would bring you the security that you craved all your life. And it worked. And now you are living a life of leisure and privilege.

But then at some point, perhaps this dream becomes a nightmare. Before it does, we must experience how your idea of security has been satisfied so that there is a context for the ensuing nightmare.

This is a moment of respite for your protagonist, when they believe that they can somehow square their desire with their inner need. It is a moment that will ultimately reveal your protagonist's ignorance or misunderstanding of their true situation. The moment of false hope is an essential aspect of your protagonist's journey, because without it, there will be no context for what is surrendered.

Until tomorrow,
Al

GROUP DISCUSSION TOPIC FOR TODAY

Do you see how your writing is influencing your creativity in other areas? Are you looking at a bare wall and imagining hanging a picture? Did you notice the way that dish at your favorite restaurant was seasoned? Did you grab a bottle of paprika or fennel seeds at the market?

WEEK 8: THOUGHTS AND REMINDERS

- This week you're writing to the point where your protagonist achieves some success, which may reveal itself to be a short-lived victory.

- If you find yourself going back and rewriting, you may be setting yourself up to get blocked later on. Keep moving forward.

- Your protagonist's decision at the end of Act One is connected to their primal desire. What is the desire? Is it for connection, meaning, purpose, success, validation, freedom, healing? Something else?

- Notice how this desire is connected to every story point. It is the beating heart of your story — and is the thing that is driving your narrative.

- Notice how the desire never changes. However, it does get reframed in Act Three.

- When your protagonist achieves success at this point in the story, notice how there's an identifiable shift for them. They have grown or changed in some identifiable way from the beginning of the story. See if you can find a way to dramatize this shift.

HOMEWORK FOR THE WEEK

1. Write a quick point-form outline from the decision at the end of Act One up to the moment of false hope. (Twenty minutes maximum.)

2. Write to the moment that your protagonist achieves an initial success (or false hope).

DAY 51

"Champions keep playing until they get it right."
—BILLIE JEAN KING

BLIND FAITH

Dear Writer,

There's an aliveness happening here for your protagonist. This is where they're exploring the new world and beginning to sense that they can conquer it. There's a new sense of possibility here, and yes, on some level it is at times terrifying, but in a different way than at the beginning. Your protagonist has made progress. They've made a decision — they're moving towards something, and this brings with it anticipation and a certain hope and possibility and wonder.

Notice as you write that you're reliving experiences that might have a very different flavor than they did when you first experienced them. But at the time, do you see how there was hope? Do you see the optimistic belief that it would all go according to plan? I mean, for God's sake, it had to!

Take us into that experience. Find the blind faith. Don't indicate where the story is going — keep us in the experience of hope.

Notice, too, that you are on a bit of a roller coaster. Wild mood swings can happen here. Do you feel a certain trembling? With hope comes the inevitable doubt. Is it going to work out? Am I going to get what I want? Will I ever find freedom or security or connection? Do you see how your protagonist is charging forward at this point in the story, fiercely determined to achieve their heart's desire?

You, the author, know that things are not going to go quite according to plan. You know there are roadblocks ahead, that there are worthy antagonists lying in wait to test your protagonist. (Otherwise there would be no story!) But your protagonist does not.

Find the hope so there can be a context for the ensuing drama.

Until tomorrow,
Al

GROUP DISCUSSION TOPIC FOR TODAY

As you begin to move into your second act, is it possible that your heart is opening just a little bit more? Do you feel a state of curiosity or wonder? Does it feel weird? Scary? Does it make you sad or angry? What is going on inside you as your protagonist begins to move into the world of Act Two? Do you feel like sharing this with your cohort group, or do you want to keep it to yourself?

DAY 52

"There is no person so severely punished, as those who subject themselves to the whip of their own remorse."   —LUCIUS ANNAEUS SENECA

REMORSE

Dear Writer,

I think of my youth, the years wasted denying my true self in an attempt to belong, pleasing people that couldn't have cared less, treating true friends carelessly, while pining for others that only caused pain.

Do you see where remorse lives in your story? It is an inevitable aspect of life, and one of the potential obstacles that can provide context for your transformation.

Notice it. Don't dine out on it, but notice where you want to turn away from it, observe the mental cartwheels that you do. Do you see how you minimize the pain caused or endured, the desire to shut it down or push it away?

Remorse can seep into us gradually over years like a steady trickle from the eaves stopped up by too many seasons of dead leaves. Or sometimes it can hit us like a hard rain.

Notice how we either rationalize our actions or we excoriate ourselves for them. What if there is a third way? What if it is possible that those years weren't wasted, that the indiscretion you had, while hurtful, was a necessary part of your growth? Perhaps it was a sincere attempt to solve a problem with the limited tools that you had at the time. What if, on some level, it was an inevitable step in your journey?

What if we discovered that the harm we caused was a byproduct of our separation from our true self? What if we accepted that we weren't mean or evil or damaged but that we simply were unable to envision the possibility of something more?

When you examine your actions from the point of view of the dilemma besetting you, as opposed to the problem you think you have, you will begin to experience some space where you previously thought you were stuck. This space is called forgiveness. Notice where it lives in your story. Notice where it holds the keys to your transformation.

Until tomorrow,
Al

GROUP DISCUSSION TOPIC FOR TODAY

Boundaries — A working artist must be able to set boundaries to protect their process. How are you respecting yourself through this process? Have you had to set a boundary with anyone recently? How did it feel? If you felt guilty, it is probably because you did the right thing!

DAY 53

"Few tragedies can be more extensive than the stunting of life, few injustices deeper than the denial of an opportunity to strive or even to hope, by a limit imposed from without, but falsely identified as lying within."   **—STEPHEN JAY GOULD**

DENIAL

Dear Writer,

We all have blind spots, those tender little lies we tell ourselves to keep us safe in the short term. Deep down you know that you're settling for less than you deserve. Or perhaps you're taking advantage of a situation that's making you feel lousy about yourself, but you don't see a way out.

Somewhere in the back of your mind is the dim awareness that one day you will pay a cost for your denial. Deep down you know that you're not standing up for yourself, that you're not speaking your truth, that you're avoiding a necessary confrontation, that your friend isn't really in your corner, that you're remaining silent out of the false belief that you'd rather settle for little than nothing at all.

Yet you wonder at the possibility that something profound awaits you, something beyond your imagination. Perhaps you're starting to glimpse a paradigm shift that reframes your struggles and a larger purpose, a method that will lead you to a clear and workable life filled with joy and peace. And then you eat a pint of ice cream and start the cycle over again.

The journey of the second act involves your protagonist tackling multiple obstacles in the form of antagonists. These characters are testing blind spots, thus forcing you to confront the things you've been afraid to look at.

You experience a brief glimpse of your true magnificence, of this deep sense of okayness, and it scares you because it is so empty of chaos and all the other things you've come to associate with being alive. Deep down you fear that true peace means losing your connection to others. The irony is that the opposite is true. Holding on is what keeps you attached to the illusion of connection, and it isn't doing any favors to the ones you think you're connected to either.

Of course, I'm not telling you anything you don't already know. But your job in the second act is to dramatize this experience, i.e., the tension between your attempt to get what you want and the antagonistic forces that are conspiring for you to surrender.

Notice the blind spots. You don't have to do anything except acknowledge their existence. As you continue through your second act, your subconscious will take care of the rest.

Until tomorrow,
Al

GROUP DISCUSSION TOPIC FOR TODAY

Fatigue — Do you feel like you're getting tired? We must learn how to rest in the midst of doing our work. Are you pacing yourself? Do you find yourself looking to the finish line? Take naps if you need them.

DAY 54

"If you want to build a ship, don't drum up people to collect wood, and don't assign them tasks and work, but rather teach them to long for the endless immensity of the sea." —ANTOINE DE SAINT EXUPÉRY

POSSIBILITY AND WONDER

Dear Writer,

We all have limitations. We need sleep. We can only tolerate so much stress. Too much work and we burn out. Being aware of one's limitations is not defeatist, it's a sign of maturity.

But when it comes to your imagination, there are no limits. Your life can actually be a constant journey of evolution. You can allow yourself to fall into that space of wonder where you are not holding onto the result, but standing in wonder at the lessons that you have learned.

When you hold onto a fixed idea of a person, place, or thing, it starts to calcify. Everything is changing, all the time, including our perceptions. This might sound weird, but our reality is changing. Have you ever believed something to be true, been convinced of it, and then suddenly, you discover that it wasn't that way at all? The journey of Act Two involves testing all of your preconceived notions in order to arrive at a place where the only thing you know for sure, is that nothing is certain. It is from this place of absolute beginning that you will be reborn in Act Three.

Until tomorrow,
Al

GROUP DISCUSSION TOPIC FOR TODAY

Did your protagonist do something today that totally surprised you? What did they say? What action did they take? Are you trusting it? Or do you find yourself saying, "My character would never do that!" Don't be so sure.

DAY 55

"Only the united beat of sex and heart together can create ecstasy."   —ANAÏS NIN, *Delta of Venus*

SEXUALITY

Dear Writer,

There is no denying it — your sexuality is likely a charged and potent element of your lived experience, and there is almost certainly a place for it in your story. One's sexuality can be used to connect but also to escape — to seduce but also to withdraw. Promiscuity and sexual anorexia are two sides of the same coin. It is also likely that you received messages very early on about what your sexuality meant, and how it was to be used.

I was raised in a strict Catholic home where sex was shrouded in mystery and shame. We had our parish priest over most Sunday nights for dinner, and as the youngest male in the family, I was somehow seen as the most eligible candidate to make my mother proud by joining the clergy. Yet even at eight, I was aware of the celibacy clause, and while I had little understanding of what sex actually entailed, I did have an instinctive sense that at some point in the future, despite my devotion to God, there was an activity that went along with my attraction to girls that I was not prepared to relinquish.

I remember one day I came home from school and my mother told me that Andrew Wilson (not his real name) was no longer allowed in our house. Andrew was a kindly doctor who worked with my father at the hospital. He lived on a nearby farm where he spent his off hours doing plein air landscape paintings, one of which hung prominently in our dining room. Andrew had gotten a divorce a few years back and had fallen in love with a new woman who had recently moved in with him. My mother wanted us all to know that God forbade sex outside of marriage, thus she had spoken with Andrew and until he married this woman, his presence in our home was prohibited.

As a twelve year old, the message to me was clear: sex was shameful, a sign of moral weakness, a cardinal sin. While I already sensed that my parents' love for me was conditional, this new bylaw reinforced an inner dread that my membership in the family was tenuous and behavior-dependent.

Notice the messages that your protagonist has received about sexuality. Notice what sex means to them, and how their relationship to sex grows, changes, or matures through the story.

Until tomorrow,
Al

GROUP DISCUSSION TOPIC FOR TODAY
Are you giving yourself permission to write poorly?

DAY 56

"Action is the antidote to despair."   —JOAN BAEZ

GROWTH

Dear Writer,

As you move into the second act of your memoir, notice how you are making choices and taking actions that you might never previously have done.

Notice how you have grown in some way from the beginning of your story. See if you can find a way to dramatize this growth by illustrating how you've changed from the beginning. For example, let's say in the beginning of your story you were afraid to commit, but by early in Act Two, you have made a commitment — and while that commitment may ultimately prove to be a painful learning experience, notice how you've changed and grown as the result of this decision.

Your goal as a storyteller is for your story to build in meaning as it progresses. Notice that as you proceed on your journey, you're learning something about yourself and the world around you. Notice how your world is more complicated than you initially believed it to be. Notice how at this point in the story your desire appears to be within reach, but that it requires a sacrifice that may put you into a compromising position.

The stakes are rising through your second act. We are becoming more invested in your journey as the result of experiencing this new growth.

Notice how you are willing to take this risk and notice the rationalizations that allow for this to happen. Notice how you tell yourself that you can make it all work, that somehow you can have your cake and eat it too. And finally, notice how there are worthy antagonists waiting in the wings to challenge this new belief.

Until tomorrow,
Al

GROUP DISCUSSION TOPIC FOR TODAY

Do you find yourself wanting to go back and edit, or are you plowing forward and giving yourself space to rewrite after you get to the end?

WEEK 9

ACT TWO:
MIDPOINT / THE POINT OF NO RETURN

This week you are writing up to the midpoint in your story. This is where your protagonist experiences temptation between what they want and what they need.

DAY 57

"The reward for conformity is that everyone likes you except yourself."   —RITA MAE BROWN

STEPPING OUT OF THE CIRCLE

Dear Writer,

Okay, this might sound weird, but while your characters are real people (obviously), flesh and blood humans who orbit your protagonist's world, they are also archetypes or primal forces whose existence allows you to explore and dramatize your dramatic question.

If this sounds like I'm suggesting that you simplify your characters or reduce them to a set of clichés, the opposite is true.

The reason we sometimes get stuck in writing our memoir is that we can become so wedded to our idea of what happened, that we fail to see the deeper truth in our story. The deeper truth involves a fundamental transformative experience for your protagonist.

Have you ever been thrown into a group of strangers, whether it is a class, a summer camp, or a new work environment? Notice how we naturally fall into roles; someone tends to ask the questions for the group, while another becomes the cheerleader, and another perhaps the moral conscience, and then there's the comic relief, the skeptic, the stubborn one, and so on. There may be some overlap, but it becomes like a Venn diagram, where we each take on a role to fill the space.

It's the same in the birth order of a family. In an attempt to get our needs met (to be loved and accepted), each child tends to instinctively play their part. For instance, you'll usually find the high achiever, the rebel, the jester, or the invisible child (yes, becoming invisible and seeming to have no needs is a strategy for being accepted). Studies suggest that we recreate these roles with alarming consistency. While each family has their own version of these archetypes, within these "roles" live fully realized characters — however, their function only becomes apparent when we understand the nature of their relationship to each other. In other words, until we recognize that we are playing a role within a system, it is impossible for us to become our truest self.

This is the goal of memoir: to become transformed by reframing our relationship to the other characters in our story by surrendering our unconscious patterns and behaviors, i.e. by stepping out of the circle.

The challenge for the memoirist is that we often have our nose pressed so closely to our notion of what happened that we sometimes miss the underlying conditions that caused the event. So this is where memoir becomes a rather strange and subversive process. When I recommend that you "hold the story loosely," I'm suggesting that your subconscious actually knows the whole truth and that it is able to make connections, discover patterns, and uncover hidden meanings. These are things that you may only fully comprehend in retrospect. This phenomenon tends to happen when we relax our grip on getting the story right, when we let go of the result.

It can be helpful to notice how all the characters in your story *all desire the same thing at nature.* Sometimes, this is a shocking revelation for the memoirist. Sometimes we are so convinced that a particular antagonist's desire is entirely at odds with our protagonist's desire, that when we see that it is actually identical, we begin to develop compassion, or at least understanding for that character. This doesn't mean that your protagonist and antagonists share the same approach to getting what they want — they don't. Their approaches vary wildly. This is what creates the conflict in your narrative.

Until tomorrow,
Al

GROUP DISCUSSION TOPIC FOR TODAY

Do you feel an impulse to talk about your work with family and friends? Is this because you're excited about your story, or perhaps anxious and wanting assurance that it makes sense? Sharing your story at this point can sometimes be self-destructive. Consider keeping your story to yourself until you complete your first draft.

WEEK 9: THOUGHTS AND REMINDERS

- This week you're writing up to the midpoint where your protagonist experiences temptation.
- The midpoint occurs as the result of an event happening that causes your protagonist to respond by committing fully to their goal.
- Be curious about your protagonist's primal desire and their dilemma. These two elements are linked. As you explore the desire and the dilemma, you will be led to a clear sense of the event that leads them to temptation.
- Committing at the midpoint is different than simply making a decision at the end of Act One. The stakes are rising. This is the point of no return. Your protagonist recognizes that there is no going back, thus leading to a moment of temptation.

- At the midpoint, be curious about how your protagonist is responding to your worthy antagonists.
- Don't worry if the narrative isn't coherent at this point. Just keep writing.
- Remember that it is not *what happens*, but the *meaning you are ascribing to what happens*, that is keeping your story compelling. Anything can be made compelling if your reader is clear on your protagonist's primal desire and the obstacles that must be overcome.

HOMEWORK FOR THE WEEK

1. Write a quick point-form outline up to the midpoint. (Twenty minutes maximum.)
2. Write to the midpoint, the moment where your protagonist commits fully to getting what they want.

DAY 58

*"The biggest human temptation is to settle for too
little."*   —THOMAS MERTON

TEMPTATION

Dear Writer,

This week you are writing up to the midpoint of your memoir,
where your protagonist experiences temptation. Notice where an
event happens somewhere in the middle of your story, and how
your protagonist responds by committing fully to their goal. Notice
where temptation lives in this commitment.

Your protagonist is tempted between what they want and what
they actually need. But it is not enough to explain this temptation
to your reader — we must experience it. So how do you dramatize
temptation? Here's how: If you know your protagonist is ultimately
going to say no to the object of their temptation, notice how they seriously consider saying yes and vice versa. In this way, your reader
will experience the *nature of the temptation* and thus meaning is
conveyed. If we don't experience your protagonist considering the
offer, there will be no context for their refusal.

Lastly, don't confuse story structure with plotting. Remember,
it is not what happens that is relevant, but rather the meaning we
ascribe to it. The midpoint moment is simply a moment where your
protagonist experiences temptation. When you take a moment or

an event from the middle of your story, and see it through the lens of temptation, you may discover that your story gets clarified.

Until tomorrow,
Al

GROUP DISCUSSION TOPIC FOR TODAY

Being a writer (which is what you are, by the way) can be thrilling and scary. How does it feel to call yourself a writer? Do you feel like a fraud, like you're not allowed to use that term because you may not have written a bestseller yet? Or does it feel like a natural part of your identity? Go look in the mirror and tell yourself you're a writer. It will make your subconscious smile.

DAY 59

"A fight is going on inside me," he said to his grand-son. "It is a terrible fight and it is between two wolves. One is evil — he is anger, envy, sorrow, regret, greed, arrogance, self-pity, guilt, resentment, inferiority, lies, false pride, superiority, and ego. The other is good — he is joy, peace, love, hope, serenity, humility, kindness, benevolence, empathy, generosity, truth, compassion, and faith. The same fight is going on in-side you — and inside every other person, too."
Grandson: "Which wolf will win?"
Grandfather: "The one you feed."
                    —NATIVE AMERICAN PARABLE

YOUR HIGHER SELF

Dear Writer,

As a teacher I'm often humbled by my students' willingness to go to the scary places. Sometimes the stories gut me and my words seem inconsequential. I'm not a therapist trained in detachment. There are days I go home and weep at the pain they've endured — home-lessness, addiction, divorce, loss of a child, a parent's suicide.

But here's something I believe: we all have a higher self — an indestructible, all-knowing self that can see around corners. This self is intuitive, it's unconditionally loving, and it always knows the right thing to do.

But it's elusive.

When you're scared or unsure of yourself, you fall into temptation and revert to your lower self. The dilemma besetting your protagonist is often the struggle between these two aspects of yourself. Remember, a dilemma is comprised of a primal desire and a false belief. It could be a desire for freedom and the false belief is the limiting idea standing in your way. The limiting idea is utterly convincing; in fact, you have mountains of evidence to support the fact that you will never be free . . .

. . .and yet, the desire for freedom persists.

You may feel yourself pulled between these two poles. You dip your toe into the pool of hope and then a setback occurs, and you retreat to the grim security of control. While it's lonely and starting to smell bad, at least it's familiar.

The thing is, and you know this — you can't control externals, your relationships, the weather, finding a parking spot, or the outcome of your memoir. And so, you find yourself — unconsciously most of the time — toggling between your higher and lower selves. Yet there's an invisible life force driving you, sometimes against your will, toward the truth. Close your eyes, take a breath — you can feel it. On a rough day you might call it fear, but on a good day you call it passion. Either way, it's just energy.

This is where your protagonist stands at this point in your story. They are at a crossroads, a point of no return, and they are being invited to trust in some invisible force to keep them going.

Imagine you're adrift in a sailboat in the middle of the ocean. Supplies are running low. There appears to be no wind. Up ahead you can see that a storm is coming, and you feel yourself starting to panic. But instead, you do what's in front of you, you put out your sail, and lo and behold a whisper of wind catches your sail and you start to move.

You have a higher self. Call it your sail.

And you have passion. That's your wind.

Something miraculous happens through this process. I've seen it too many times not to trust it. In fact, I don't believe it ever fails, and even though it seems to make no logical sense, that's because we aren't supposed to know yet what we aren't supposed to know yet.

Your protagonist doesn't have the answer but they know one thing — there's no going back. This is your point of no return. You may not be able to see dry land but you're moving in that direction. A storm most certainly is coming and you are about to be tested.

Trust that you are being guided to a greater freedom. And while you can never figure your way out to your liberation, maybe the answer you're seeking doesn't live in your head.

Take the risk. Trust your sail. Trust that your higher self is the captain and we are your passengers. We are depending on you to get us home.

Until tomorrow,
Al

GROUP DISCUSSION TOPIC FOR TODAY

Being a writer is an act of self-love. What are you going to do today to thank your subconscious for doing all this brilliant work for you on your behalf?

DAY 60

"There are no passengers on spaceship earth. We are all crew."   —Marshall McLuhan

FINDING YOUR "NO"

Dear Writer,

Writing a memoir is a bold act. It's not merely an examination and/or a dramatization of your life, but an admission that you deserve to take up space, that what you have to express is valid, thus it has the potential to be of value to others.

Notice, as you move into the second half of Act Two, how the stakes are rising for your protagonist as they are beginning to recognize that what appeared to be a problem is becoming a dilemma. One way of looking at it is this: "Will I take up space and disrupt the status quo or will I conform and lose myself in the process?"

Do you see where this experience lives in your story?

There's a scene in the middle of the movie *It's a Wonderful Life* where the villain, Mr. Potter, realizes he can't defeat George Bailey, and so, he offers him a job in an attempt to pull him over to his side. This is George Bailey's point of no return moment. After considering the offer (his moment of temptation), he suddenly realizes that he's being asked to make a deal with the devil, and he says, "No!" It is the moment he recognizes that even if his dreams are dashed, he cannot afford to lose his soul.

Your protagonist is growing. They're confronting obstacles, and you're probably noticing at this point in your story that they've learned something about themselves that they didn't know before. Do you see how they're willing to trust themselves on some fundamental level? Perhaps they're willing to feel that rage and not bury it in excuses, rationalizations, or denial.

Notice how your protagonist is no longer willing to say yes when the answer is no and if they do say yes, how their body registers this self-betrayal. Something has been awakened, and damn it, it isn't going back to sleep!

So does this mean you're nearing the end of your story? No! More trouble lies ahead, because while your protagonist is growing stronger and more savvy in one sense, they've yet to discover the true nature of their struggle. But more on that later.

Let's do an exercise to find that "No" in your body. Shut the door, shut the windows, turn off your phone. Take three deep breaths and locate that "No" inside of you.

Shout it to the heavens. Go ahead. Hit a pillow for God's sake. "No! No! No! No!"

Do you feel foolish? Good. Keep doing it until you don't. Your protagonist is going to need this fire to get to the end of Act Two.

Until tomorrow,
Al

GROUP DISCUSSION TOPIC FOR TODAY

Do you find yourself beating yourself up? *I'm not doing it right. I've fallen behind. This isn't any good.* What is your negative voice saying today? Write it down. Notice where it lives for your protagonist in the story. Notice how you are not the author, but the channel. Notice how your subconscious is the seat of your genius. Notice how you alone are uniquely qualified (because of your struggles!) to write this brilliant story.

DAY 61

"Come back! Even as a shadow, even as a dream."
                                        —EURIPIDES

WRITING FROM YOUR BROKEN HEART

Dear Writer,

As we move more deeply into the middle section of our story, we notice that we are getting distracted. Suddenly our home is becoming cleaner — we're doing laundry and washing windows, and doing just about anything to avoid having to write.

As we continue writing, we are vaguely aware that we are marching our protagonist towards a brick wall. Even if they win, they lose. There is no way around the fact that our conscious goal is actually, ironically, preventing us from achieving our heart's desire. There is no away around the fact that we are moving inexorably toward the death of something that, while perhaps not quite working, is deeply familiar — so familiar, in fact, that we may have mistaken it for our true identity.

But there is magic in story, just like there is in life. And sometimes it comes from the most unexpected place. When we write from our broken heart, we let go of the delusion that anything out there in the world can fix anything within. When we write from our broken heart, our big goal can seem sort of insignificant, like a cosmic speck.

I don't mean to suggest that it isn't important, but only that in relation to your inner need (the peace and serenity that are your birthright), your goal must take a backseat.

While your protagonist is still actively pursuing their goal with unbridled abandon, see if you can allow your heart to break just a little bit in relation to this goal. See if you can allow yourself to loosen your grip on your goal. This isn't giving up. This is letting go of the false belief that your outward goal can ever fulfill your heart's desire. The irony is that until you let it go, you will only ever be in bondage to it anyway.

Until tomorrow,
Al

GROUP DISCUSSION TOPIC FOR TODAY

Do you see where the dilemma lives for your protagonist in the midpoint?

DAY 62

"My mission in life is not merely to survive, but to thrive; and to do so with some passion, some compassion, some humor, and some style"
—MAYA ANGELOU

SURVIVAL

Dear Writer,

Your protagonist is in search of a truth that will liberate them from their struggle. The irony is that the survival strategy they are employing to combat their struggle is the very thing that is standing between themselves and a greater freedom. And while these strategies may prove quite effective in the short term, notice how they are standing in the way of your protagonist's transformation.

We all have survival strategies to keep ourselves safe, but these strategies can also prevent us from growing. Your memoir is an illustration of your internal growth. As you move toward the end of the second section in your story, notice how your protagonist is moving inexorably towards confronting this truth.

Notice how all your characters desire the same thing at their core. While their approaches may be in complete opposition, they all constellate around the same dilemma. This is because their mutual desire will lead to a deeper truth regarding the theme. Imagine the conflict that arises as two characters each pursue a mutual desire through opposing means. Here are some examples:

- SECURITY: One character may seek security by sharing their feelings while their partner may seek security by hiding their feelings.
- FREEDOM: One character believes that freedom comes from making lots of money, while another character believes that freedom comes from relinquishing all worldly possessions.
- MEANING: One character might search for meaning through external channels, e.g. career, relationships, notoriety, acquisition, while another might find meaning through an inward search.

Until tomorrow,
Al

GROUP DISCUSSION TOPIC FOR TODAY

As you approach the midpoint, do you see how you are being invited to "commit fully" to the story? How does that feel? Is it exciting? Does it feel like a big responsibility? Do you see how you must let go of having to figure it all out if you are to get to the end?

DAY 63

"You must not lose faith in humanity. Humanity is an ocean; if a few drops of the ocean are dirty, the ocean does not become dirty."

—MAHATMA GANDHI

HUMANITY

Dear Writer,

When a writer shares their work in class and it involves a challenge, an obstacle, a painful experience, when they share their flaws, their weaknesses, or failings . . . we lean in. Why? Because we've all wrestled with our own conscience. We've all made mistakes, and we carry the shame and the scars to prove it. And when someone has the courage to share what they believe makes them weak, we often admire them for their bravery.

Notice how your vulnerability moves us towards you. And notice how, through your struggle, we are relying on you to offer us some clues that will lead us out of our own struggle. While we may not relate to your identical experience, we relate to the nature of it. We all understand loss, abandonment, betrayal, or innocence violated; however, you will likely notice in your memoir how you are an authority on one of these themes. Notice how your experience has blessed you with the dubious honor of becoming an expert on loss, for instance. But your memoir is not merely an account of a particular painful event; it also delineates your journey out of this circumstance or at least shows us how you managed to reframe your relationship to this experience.

Look at the title of Joan Didion's memoir, *The Year of Magical Thinking.* She didn't call it *My Life of Magical Thinking.* Instead, her transformation is implied in the title. The title refers to the human survival instinct to retreat into fantasy to deal with a terrible loss. Suffering the loss of her husband while her daughter lies in a coma, she is going to track her experience of magical thinking. She can't throw out the shoes of her dead husband because she is expecting him to return. He will need them. She is going to track the dilemma besetting her, i.e. how her unwillingness to accept his death is preventing her from living in reality while at the same time concerned that reality itself may be too unbearable to endure.

As human beings we do not like to change. We will do anything to avoid it. What makes memoirists brave is that we are exposing our pain in order to reframe it in a way that conveys a transformation for the reader.

It's important to note that transformation doesn't mean enlightenment. The story doesn't necessarily end with you sitting on a mountaintop, with the warm breeze of truth blowing through your tresses. It simply means that you understand something at the end that you didn't understand at the beginning, that you have somehow, perhaps in the smallest way, integrated the painful experience(s) from your life and made new meaning out of them.

We understand that you can never go back to the way things were, that you will be forever changed because of this experience. Notice how your magical thinking keeps you wanting to return to the scene of the crime, to find a way to do it differently. What if the way out is accepting that things will never be the same again? What if you lean into your broken heart and discover, ironically, that this is where your common humanity lives, that freedom doesn't come from being free of your pain, but from accepting it.

Until tomorrow,
Al

GROUP DISCUSSION TOPIC FOR TODAY

You are approaching the midway point in your first draft. If you're not there yet, don't panic or rush to *catch up*. Are you noticing that as you continue this work, the highs and lows tend to level out (a little bit)? You just can't get too worked up about the breakthroughs or the apparent setbacks. Are you beginning to sense that you are simply a channel for this story that is passing through you?

WEEK 10

ACT TWO:
YOUR PROTAGONIST SUFFERS

This week you are writing up to the point where your protagonist suffers in their attempt to achieve their goal. While it may appear that on some level your protagonist is continually suffering, this experience is directly related to their dilemma. This is sometimes a moment where they must dig their heels in and put on blinders. This is their last chance to get what they want based on their current approach (or their false belief on how they think their freedom should look).

DAY 64

"Don't take anything personally. Nothing others do is because of you. What others say and do is a projection of their own reality, their own dream. When you are immune to the opinions and actions of others, you won't be the victim of needless suffering."
—DON MIGUEL RUIZ

IT WASN'T PERSONAL

Dear Writer,

How on earth do we not take it personally? These things that were done to us! Monstrous things! They are real! They happened. They caused us great pain. How can you say it wasn't personal? It was done with aforethought. It was calculated! It was premeditated. It was cruel and unfair and unforgiveable.

But also this: If you were someone else, it would still have happened. It wasn't done to You with a capital Y. It was done to you.

How do we become immune to the opinions of others?

It happens over time. Forgiveness isn't something we do for others; it is something we do for ourselves. We aren't forgiving the act that was committed; we are forgiving the meaning that we have made out of it — that we are broken, that we should never have put ourselves in that position, that we played a part in it.

Until we forgive ourselves, we will carry the pain. The lesson is simple. We never have to be a victim again if we don't want to be.

Modern culture tells us to follow our bliss or dare to be extraordinary — implying that you aren't already or that "extraordinary" is a verb and not a noun. You were born extraordinary. It's subtly shaming, implying that you're not yet enough. It's a marketing strategy to sell you a lifestyle that will only distract you from what you actually need.

Yes, you are the protagonist in your memoir, but it is not about you. It is about your relationship to the outside world. You cannot experience a transformation without conflict or tension with other human beings. It is only through this process that you can be led to some kind of new understanding of your situation.

Until tomorrow,
Al

GROUP DISCUSSION TOPIC FOR TODAY

Are you allowing yourseltf to be surprised with where the characters are taking you?

WEEK 10: THOUGHTS AND REMINDERS

- This week you are writing up to the point where your protagonist suffers.
- Your story isn't a linear journey. Your protagonist's trajectory shifts as a result of their attempt to achieve their goal.
- Your protagonist's goal doesn't change. However, their approach to it is always shifting.
- Your protagonist suffers as they begin to recognize the difficulty of ever getting what they want. See if you can

find that experience of, "Oh God, I had no idea it was going to be this difficult."

- Suffering is different than surrender. When you suffer, you tend to dig your heels in or put blinders on. You suffer because things are difficult. You surrender because things are impossible.

- Surrender: the next major beat in your protagonist's journey happens as the result of letting go of their "want." Your protagonist still desires the same goal; it's just that they recognize that their desire is preventing them from attaining it.

- If this moment feels unclear, be curious about your worthy antagonists. Every time your protagonist attempts to get what they want, they are faced with new obstacles.

HOMEWORK FOR THE WEEK

1. Write a quick point-form outline up to the moment our protagonist suffers. (Twenty minutes maximum.)

2. Write to the moment your protagonist suffers.

DAY 65

"The most authentic thing about us is our capacity to create, to overcome, to endure, to transform, to love, and to be greater than our suffering."

—BEN OKRI

SUFFERING

Dear Writer,

There is no question that the experience of suffering will find its way into your memoir. It is an essential aspect of the human experience and a necessary one if there is to be a surrender. Your protagonist's suffering will provide context for their letting go.

Notice where the experience of suffering happens in your story and notice, too, the nature of this suffering because it is directly related to your protagonist's dilemma.

If your protagonist is to reframe their relationship to their struggle, they must first die to their old identity, their limiting belief of themselves or the world. The experience of suffering arrives as the result of committing fully to one's goal and it is the inflection point that leads to their eventual surrender. Think about any commitment that you've made in your life, from the decision to get married, to the decision to get up at 5:00 a.m. to begin your marathon training. Notice that, however small, there is a hesitation, a resistance, a questioning of why you ever committed to this thing in the first place.

As human beings, we do not like change. We resist it. Even positive change can stir us up and create turmoil in our lives. Look at all the stories of lottery winners whose lives were upended after their windfall. As much as you may resist the idea of suffering, notice where your protagonist (as the result of committing fully to their goal) resists the inevitable change that comes with it. Any change is a shock to the system, and that is what is happening for your protagonist at this point in your story.

Perhaps your protagonist is facing something that they have avoided. Perhaps they are making choices that are leading them further into isolation. Perhaps they are agreeing to things that no longer feel okay, but they have yet to choose a new path. Or perhaps your protagonist is moving on and starting a new life. Regardless of the event, notice how your protagonist is moving inexorably toward a condition of suffering.

Until tomorrow,
Al

GROUP DISCUSSION TOPIC FOR TODAY

As a result of committing to their goal, do you see how your protagonist is moving towards suffering? What is your relationship to this experience in your life today? Have you ever noticed that it is only after we fully commit to anything that we must endure sincere struggle in order to be transformed?

DAY 66

"What is full of redundancy or formula is predictably boring. What is free of all structure or discipline is randomly boring. In between lies art."
—**WENDY CARLOS**

REPETITION

Dear Writer,

In our lives, we often repeat patterns, doing the same thing over and over and expecting a different result. However, in memoir, the challenge is to convey the experience of reality while not burdening the reader with meaningless repetition. This doesn't mean you can't repeat an action — like a character returning to a bad relationship for the fifth time — however, the meaning we ascribe to the action must be different each time.

Notice how each return elicits a different response — each return has a slightly different flavor, each return is saying something new. Redundancy at the level of meaning will only bore your reader. Once it has been said, you must move on.

Sometimes, as we move more deeply into our narrative, we find ourselves circling the airport, revisiting the issue from the same place, without advancing the narrative. Even if the events are different, even if the scene now takes place at the cottage rather than the coffee shop, the stakes don't seem to be rising, the story doesn't seem to be building in meaning as it progresses because the struggle has not changed in a fundamental way.

Remember that character is revealed through action. By putting your protagonist into conflict, meaning will be conveyed.

What is the obstacle going on for your protagonist right now in this scene that demands an urgent response? Take a breath and write it down. While you know the facts of this event, allow yourself to be surprised by the insights that emerge.

Until tomorrow,
Al

GROUP DISCUSSION TOPIC FOR TODAY
What are you doing today to reward yourself?

DAY 67

"Life is a series of natural and spontaneous changes. Don't resist them — that only creates sorrow. Let reality be reality. Let things flow naturally forward in whatever way they like."   **—LAO TZU**

MEMOIR IS A DIALOGUE

Dear Writer,

As writers, we work alone. It is a solitary journey as we traverse the narrow, sometimes rocky path of our psyche.

Yet, the truth is that your memoir is a dialogue between you and your ideal reader. Imagine them sitting quietly in the corner of your room, forever asking "Why?" — forever seeking to make meaning out of your experiences.

"Why did you say no to such an irresistible offer?"

"Were you really in love with Dan or were you just trying to escape your family?"

"How did you cope with the death of your dog?"

And so on.

When you approach your memoir from this place, you begin to connect to your ally, your inner reader. Sometimes we take the events of our life for granted. We assume that everyone understands the nature of our struggle.

They don't.

I'll have a writer say, "I got a divorce." And I'll say, "What does that mean?" And they might get huffy and say, "It was the worst event of my life," or they might laugh and say, "It was such a relief to get out of that marriage," or maybe, "I never really loved _____."

Story is not about what happens, but about the meaning you ascribe to what happens. As you write, pay attention to your ideal reader sitting in the corner asking questions.

Until tomorrow,
Al

GROUP DISCUSSION TOPIC FOR TODAY

This is the week to be really gentle with yourself while getting your writing done. Is there something you can take off your "To Do" list today?

DAY 68

"If you're going through hell, keep going."
—**WINSTON CHURCHILL**

KEEP GOING

Dear Writer,

If you're feeling a certain heaviness in the process right now, please know this will likely pass very soon. You're taking your protagonist down the long dark corridor toward surrender, and it probably feels like you're lugging a bag of rocks on your shoulder. It can feel lonely and scary as you revisit events from the past that may feel better left unremembered. Perhaps there are tears. Let them flow.

You're not doing this alone. You're united by a family of writers who share your search for some kind of truth — one that doesn't prop you up with sweet sentimentality and false promises. Yes, it hurts sometimes. There's no question that this process invites grief. But when you let it flow through you and trust that you're not alone, you'll discover that you're being carried to higher ground.

Remember, you're not the author, you're the channel. Your job is to listen and take dictation — even if the words you're putting on the page surprise or disturb you. Give yourself permission to write this first draft for yourself. You can edit it later.

Sometimes simply knowing that you don't have to show this to anyone allows you to go to the places you need to go. And you may be surprised to find when you get to the end that you have a new relationship to what you thought was forbidden.

To be human is to endure suffering, but through your memoir you're making meaning out of the suffering. Without these challenges, there would be nothing to surrender, and without surrender, there can be no transformation.

Stay with it. You're waking up to something. You're being led to a greater freedom. You will be on the other side soon, and you'll likely understand your situation in a way that you never previously imagined.

Until tomorrow,
Al

GROUP DISCUSSION TOPIC FOR TODAY

What is one thing you would like to let go of in your life? Is there one thing standing between you and a sense of peace?

DAY 69

*"The greatest shortcoming of the human race is our
inability to understand the exponential function."*
—**ALBERT ALLEN BARTLETT**, *physicist*

DON'T QUIT BEFORE THE MIRACLE

Dear Writer,

Whether it is compound interest, bacterial growth, cell division,
or the degrading of radioactive matter, the exponential function is
a naturally occurring phenomenon that describes the exponential
growth or decay of a given set of data.

Here's what I'm getting at: in the early stages of any endeavor,
it can be difficult to identify one's growth and the temptation to
throw in the towel can emerge. What this means in terms of your
writing is that while you might experience your growth as incre-
mental in terms of putting words on the page, I believe it is exponential in terms of the wisdom you're accruing.

Consider the effect in mathematical terms: $2 \times 2 = 4$. $4 \times 4 =
16$. $16 \times 16 = 256$. In the early stages the numbers are relatively
small, but if each day we multiplied the product, notice what happens on Day Four. The number jumps to 65,536. If you graphed it
you would see the curve suddenly turn into an almost vertical line.
This is the exponential effect. Day Five is almost 4.3 billion!

But even with exponential growth, it never moves in a straight
line. There are downticks and sometimes these downticks can feel

like major setbacks. It's important to remember that they're temporary. Don't make too much meaning out of them. Don't confuse sadness or even despair with a permanent state. Writing may appear to be a placid, sedentary activity but it isn't. In memoir, you are, to some degree, reliving experiences that are inviting you to examine and reframe their meaning. You are moving out of victimhood and this can bring up all sorts of big feelings. Two steps forward, one step back.

With each passing day you're building an inner core by developing a coherent narrative, and while it is human nature to chase short-term gratification, the long-term benefits of staying with your truth are beyond our human capacity to imagine. We tend to think in terms of being powered by our own steam, but when you engage in the creative process you're tapping into something larger than you. You're connecting to your Higher Self which is a portal to the wisdom of the ages. Yes, this is brave work, but the work that makes you tremble with fear today becomes a no-brainer tomorrow.

I believe our human capacity for compassion, forgiveness, joy, and self-worth is infinite. I believe our potential for true freedom and wisdom is beyond the limited ability of our left brain to comprehend. Your left brain is logical. It sees things in practical terms but it also only understands the world from your old limiting beliefs and hang ups, those guilt-ridden messages passed down to you from your ancestors. It will never have a frame of reference for what is truly possible. If you argue with your left brain, it will always win, but that doesn't make it correct.

Your subconscious is the seat of your genius. It has access to your Higher Self and this is where the exponential function resides. It's not supposed to make sense, at least not logically. There's a deeper truth that may not entirely make sense at this point in your journey but weirdly, when you get to the end, it will become self-evident. Despite this broken world we're inhabiting, the universe is love and it is this law to which the human animal will ultimately always bend.

Don't stop. Trust your tiny breakthroughs today. Trust the exponential function because while it may feel minor, you are marching toward freedom.

Until tomorrow,
Al

GROUP DISCUSSION TOPIC FOR TODAY

What is your greatest fear? Write it down in one sentence. Can you, just for a moment, entertain the possibility that while you have a mountain of data to support the fear, it might still be based on a false premise?

DAY 70

"Nothing dies harder than a bad idea."

—JULIA CAMERON

BAGGAGE

Dear Writer,

We all have baggage. We lug it around because it protects us in the short run. And while it may not be serving us, it sure feels familiar. Notice the bad idea that your protagonist is carrying around with them. This is merely a limiting idea they have of themselves or the world. It is this idea that will be surrendered at the end of Act Two.

It seems like it should be easy to let go of a bad idea, but notice how loyal we can be to these often unexamined nuggets of turd.

There's a term I heard a while back: learned helplessness. Notice where your protagonist doesn't see a way out of their situation. It's a like a rat in those psychological experiments that gets shocked every time they try to leave the cage, and so, even after the cage door is opened and the electricity is turned off, they stay in their cage, even willing to die of hunger so as not to risk being shocked one more time.

Notice where this fear lives for your protagonist. Notice where they are so convinced by the appearance of their situation that they are not yet willing to drop their old belief.

What is the risk that needs to be taken? What is the difficult choice standing between your protagonist and their authentic life? Notice how your protagonist believes that they could die if they actually take the risk of leaving an abusive relationship, of being vulnerable, of speaking their truth. Notice the fixed idea or false belief that your protagonist is going to surrender in order to be free.

Until tomorrow,
Al

GROUP DISCUSSION TOPIC FOR TODAY

What is the fear that your protagonist is walking through at this point in your story? What is your relationship to this fear in your life today?

WEEK 11

ACT TWO:
YOUR PROTAGONIST SURRENDERS

This week your protagonist is going to surrender. They are going to recognize the impossibility of getting what they want based on their current approach, and they are going to let go.

DAY 71

"I tore myself away from the safe comfort of certainties through my love for truth — and truth rewarded me."   —SIMONE DE BEAUVOIR

THE TRUTH

Dear Writer,

Your memoir is a search for the truth. This search transcends blame and shame.

The truth is not a fixed point but neither is it a moving target. Through patience and sincere inquiry, your relationship to the truth grows. The truth welcomes argument and discourse and it is never defensive. What is there to defend? The truth, if valued and respected, deepens with age. It's like the wood grain in a fine oak table that has weathered the seasons; it takes on a patina, a depth and richness. The truth welcomes tension and conflict because it only adds to its understanding. You can try to hide from the truth, throw stones at it, deny it, rationalize it, persuade it, cajole it, bargain with it, seduce it, manipulate it, threaten it, ignore it, punish it, humiliate it, berate it, deprive it. But ultimately, it is like those Weebles we played with as a kid; they wobble but they don't fall down.

The truth is impervious. You can try to kill it but it would be like trying to kill the stars. The truth is in all of us — it is our natural resting state, absent of fear — in fact, the notion of truth only ever rears its head when we realize that we're not living it. Only then do we feel it as a creeping unease, where we recognize that we've rationalized our choice but deep down know that we can never outrun it.

When you sit quietly and listen to your inner voice, you know what the truth is. You don't need a guru or a therapy session or a yoga class. You just need to notice where you flinch.

Do you see where this experience lives for your protagonist?

As your protagonist moves toward surrender, notice that letting go is a necessary step towards waking up to the truth. The truth usually comes to us incrementally over time, but sometimes it arrives like a pugilist, almost shocking in its brutal bluntness. It comes in the form of a betrayal, a terrible loss, or a sudden involuntary moment where the universe grabs us by the throat and tells us to wake up. Ultimately, the truth is never unkind, though it can be terribly inconvenient.

The truth tells you:

- "You've outgrown this relationship. Stop waiting for them to change."
- "You are more resilient than you think."
- "You owe that person an apology."
- "You don't owe that person an apology."
- "Don't worry, your vulnerability isn't going to kill you."
- "You need to be alone right now."
- "You can take the risk of telling them you love them."
- "You're allowed to change your mind."
- "Their anger doesn't mean you've done something wrong. And if you have, you can take responsibility without excoriating yourself."
- "You actually don't want that promotion. In fact, you don't really want that career."
- "You need a nap."
- "You are forgiven."

Take a breath and listen. The truth is always pointing you in the direction you need to go. And the truth, while it may be disruptive, is always guiding you to freedom.

Until tomorrow,
Al

GROUP DISCUSSION TOPIC FOR TODAY

What are three things that your protagonist values? When you imagine them being removed, do you see how that takes you to their dark night of the soul experience?

WEEK 11: THOUGHTS AND REMINDERS

- Suffering is the final gasp that leads your protagonist to their moment of surrender.

- We surrender only when we recognize the impossibility of ever getting what we want.

- When your protagonist surrenders, they reframe their idea of what they want.

- Your protagonist surrenders because they suddenly realize that they are not struggling with a problem but with a dilemma.

- Until your protagonist reframes their relationship to their goal, there can be no transformation.

- Your story asks everything of you for a reason. If it didn't, you would never surrender your fixed idea about yourself or the world. The good news is that in surrendering, you are always led to greater freedom, more love, and an absence of shame.

- There is a difference between your protagonist's surrender at the end of Act Two and the climax/battle scene at the end of Act Three. Your protagonist surrenders because they have no choice. The battle scene involves making a new choice. Your protagonist makes a new choice at the end, thus proving to the gods they have earned their shift in perception.

HOMEWORK FOR THE WEEK

1. Write a quick point-form outline to the end of Act Two. (Twenty minutes maximum.)
2. Write to the moment where your protagonist surrenders.

DAY 72

"Beauty begins the moment you decide to be
yourself."   —COCO CHANEL

LETTING GO

Dear Writer,

How is it that we can so easily see the beauty in others but we so often struggle to see it in ourselves? How is it that someone in the workshop can share a writing exercise — a toss off — that leaves us speechless, while they fail to see the profundity of what they just did?

"What?" they say, "I just wrote down what happened!"

No, what happened was channeled through your empathic imagination, and through some alchemical process, art was created!

It is sometimes hard to fathom how your fundamental ordinariness, stripped of artifice, can be so breathtaking to others. It is hard to comprehend the fact that there is no one else like you — and that that alone is your superpower.

My father ran a private psychiatric hospital for twenty years, and each Christmas, before we opened our presents, he took us to visit the aging patients on Ward C. Many of them were near death, sitting lifeless, medicated, nodding off or staring into space. But when we entered the ward, they turned as if drawn by some magnetic force to our childlike innocence, their eyes widened and something awakened in them — it was alarming, this palpable desire for connection. Some of them shrieked when we held their hands.

It is difficult to comprehend the inherent power that you possess but also, how fragile that power is. The irony is that your power radiates from you when you're in your truth and yet it is so easy to dim your light by trying to be something other than who you are.

This week you're moving in the direction of stepping into your true power by shedding the false belief that that power ever came from a source outside of yourself. But this shedding involves a death — a death of your protagonist's old identity. The Phoenix must die before it rises from the ashes. You don't actually have to do anything; nothing is required of you except to let go, to breathe, and to trust that all you are leaving behind is the false belief that you are not enough.

To live in a state of wonder, of joy, of immeasurable gratitude for the simple fact that you are here — right now — in the midst of all this turmoil and upheaval. Here you are and you can do something. You can say something. You have a voice and you can express something authentic that may perhaps move this broken world one step closer to peace. It isn't going to happen with politicians and world leaders, or even scientists. The world can only heal when we tell ourselves a new story — and that story involves a surrender of the old one.

This week you're letting go of the old story.

The old story is that you require external validation before you can soar, that you're forever in bondage to your past, that you can never move on from trauma, that you're unworthy of love, that you can never be forgiven, that you need to become something *better* than who you are — in fact, that is the lie that's been keeping you stuck.

The great irony is that your "flaw" holds the keys to your miraculous new self. André Gide said, "Loving yourself isn't vanity. It's sanity."

Surrender does not mean giving up; it means letting go of the meaning you made out of your goal. Surrender is the end of a limiting belief that you had about yourself or the world. It is where your perspective widens, where you understand what you were avoiding and your dilemma becomes apparent.

This week you are moving towards an experience of surrender. Be gentle with yourself. Without surrender, there can be no transformation.

Until tomorrow,
Al

GROUP DISCUSSION TOPIC FOR TODAY

Be open to surprises here. When your protagonist considers giving up, do you see how this is related to their dilemma? Be specific about *what* they are considering giving up. It may be slightly different than what you thought it was.

DAY 73

"Your purpose is to be yourself. You don't have to run anywhere to become someone else. You are wonderful just as you are."   **—Thich Nhat Hanh**

FREEDOM IS YOUR BIRTHRIGHT

Dear Writer,

Freedom is your birthright. But sometimes the cost of true freedom involves being stripped of the external trappings we falsely believed provided us with our identity. Don't worry. I'm not suggesting you move to the nearest mountaintop and spend the rest of your days in quiet seclusion, but I am suggesting this: as you move toward the end of your second act, notice how your protagonist has been holding onto a fixed idea that they believed provided them with security and notice how that idea may, in fact, be the root cause of their suffering.

The challenge is that it can be difficult to see what you're holding onto when you may not be aware that you're holding onto anything. And quite often, the thing your protagonist is holding onto provides them with a temporary payoff — they get to be right, or angry, or certain of something, or they get to justify their position as a victim. Isn't it interesting how our contempt, superiority, self-righteousness and self-pity can provide us with the illusion of power and control while at the same time keeping us isolated from others and keeping freedom at bay? In other words, *notice how your desire prevents you from achieving your goal.*

But what if your protagonist doesn't know the whole story? What if the meaning they make out of their suffering is misguided? What if they were able to step out of the victim role?

This week, notice how the stakes are rising and how it is becoming increasingly difficult to ignore the truth that the meaning your protagonist makes out of their goal holds within it the seed of their inevitable surrender.

Until tomorrow,
Al

GROUP DISCUSSION TOPIC FOR TODAY

Have you heard the term "toxic positivity"? Have you ever spent time around someone who is so pathologically positive that you sense they're disconnected from themselves? It's not uplifting — in fact, it's the opposite. It's disconcerting. You actually start to feel uncomfortable around them, like they're hiding something. It seems like they're unable to express or integrate these "bad feelings" — their sadness, grief, or despair. Have you noticed that when you're in your true power you can hold a space for these heavier feelings without getting sidelined? That these feelings can actually deepen your experience of life? That your true power lies not in pretending to be in control but in your willingness to be vulnerable?

DAY 74

"The most beautiful people we have known are those who have known defeat, known suffering, known struggle, known loss, and have found their way out of the depths. These persons have an appreciation, a sensitivity, and an understanding of life that fills them with compassion, gentleness, and a deep loving concern. Beautiful people do not just happen."
—**Dr. Elisabeth Kübler-Ross**

RAGE AND GRIEF

Dear Writer,

Your search for the truth often elicits the dual experiences of rage and grief. One flows into the other, and then back again. As you write, you may have insights that unlock deep-seated emotions. You may think, "Why did I allow that to happen?!" or "How could I have done such a thing?!" The anger burns in your chest, violent and white hot, and as the heat cools, it is often followed by grief and regret.

Sometimes, our impulse is to back away from this experience. These feelings can scare us. But what if you leaned into it, took a closer look and discovered that within the grief was a gift? What if the gift is a sort of wisdom — a wider perspective? What if your memoir shines a light on your journey out of some kind of darkness and leads you back to a deeper connection to others?

Do you see how your experience, while painful at times, gives you the credibility to shine a light for the rest of us? You know something we don't. Your pain can be transmuted into an insight that helps others.

We all have pain. When we deny it, or pretend it wasn't such a big deal, it gets suppressed and works its way into the marrow of our bones. But if you take the risk of putting your truth on the page, an alchemical process starts to happen. It's sort of like chelation therapy, in which a substance is used to bind metals so they can be excreted from the body. Have you ever read a novel or memoir that moved you deeply, that transformed you in some way? Do you see how the act of writing your story is forming a connection between you and your future readers that can set both of you free? The pain of your past is exorcised and transformed into power, a beacon that guides your reader through the treacherous waters of their own experience and in some mysterious way sets both of you free.

Until tomorrow,
Al

GROUP DISCUSSION TOPIC FOR TODAY

You may be feeling discouraged. This is a common state at this point in the process. Ask yourself this: What am I being invited to let go of?

DAY 75

"Our uniqueness makes us special, . . . but it can also make us lonely."   —AMY TAN

SPECIAL

Dear Writer,

We all want to be special.

The desire to be special is encoded in our DNA. It's a primal drive attached to our survival instinct. In caveman days, being special significantly improved your chances of making it to adulthood — it meant you were loved and therefore you were fed and clothed and your needs were met. Being special meant you were more likely to thrive.

We live in a celebrity-obsessed culture where popularity is mistaken for authenticity, where optics trump integrity, where perception is a substitute for true value and, at least subconsciously, one's perceived "specialness" is defined by the reach of their social media presence or digital market share.

We seem to have fallen under the collective delusion that our self-worth is defined by others, and this desire can become a way of chasing short-term gratification as a distraction from pursuing your heart's desire. And while it can be pleasant, and a temporary boost to your ego in the form of compliments and accolades, it can also be a slippery slope. It can lead you to make choices based on the desire to be loved and approved of rather than the choice to create something lasting and meaningful.

Being true to yourself can be terrifying, confusing, and lonely, and it can sometimes piss people off. It often means that you must deepen your resolve and accept the possibility that you could fail in your goal. Perhaps true failure is measured by the chasm we create between our authentic selves and the social mask we've created in our attempts to get more of what we don't need.

As your protagonist approaches their dark night of the soul, this is where they may begin to discover that in running towards their goal, they've actually run away from their heart's desire. In one way or another, they may see that they've been pursuing the wrong thing.

In Cheryl Strayed's *Wild*, she realizes that she doesn't need to be tougher or stronger but rather she needs to grieve the losses she's been trying to outrun. This is scary and lonely and it can feel like too much to ask of ourselves.

But what if your protagonist reframed their relationship to this desire? What if they approached it as if it was not an either/or proposition? Because here's the thing: your desire to be special is probably never going away. In fact, there is nothing inherently wrong with it as long as it takes its rightful place as a motivator to get you going but not as the driving force for your decisions.

The secret is to put your protagonist's need before their want (i.e., their need to fulfill their heart's desire before their wish to be accepted).

This is the point you're approaching this week. Do you see how your protagonist's desire to be special may be at odds with their need to be true to themselves? Do you see how this desire is reaching a crescendo, how external forces are conspiring to bring your protagonist to their knees? As long as your protagonist is looking outside of themselves for something to fulfill an inner need, they will forever be in bondage to external forces.

Notice where this experience lives for your protagonist in the story. What is your protagonist holding onto? Notice how it is in celebrating their ordinariness that they will discover what makes them unique, and they will be set free.

Until tomorrow,
Al

GROUP DISCUSSION TOPIC FOR TODAY

You're approaching the dark night of the soul. What can you do for yourself today that feels like an indulgence? It could be as simple as taking yourself for a half-hour walk in nature. Remember, being an artist requires regular acts of self-love. How are you being kind to yourself today?

DAY 76

"Life begins on the other side of despair."
—JEAN PAUL SARTRE

CRY INTO THE VOID

Dear Writer,

The cry into the void is your protagonist's anguished shriek that leads to the surrender of everything they thought they valued. The end of Act Two is like a coin with two sides. On one side is despair and on the other side is a new hope, a wider perspective. The facts of your protagonist's situation do not change but their relationship to these facts does a 180-degree turn, and suddenly, what was the lowest moment in their life becomes the springboard to face their situation from a place of true power.

We typically approach our lives with statements of gusto. "Grab the bull by the horns," or "Seize the day." Notice how we tend to view living a grand life as holding on tightly. Look at how each of the statements below can get reframed by simply seeing them as an opportunity to let go.

EXAMPLES:
- "All is lost." (So now I can finally start over.)
- "I'm all alone." (So I no longer have to abandon myself to fit in.)
- "Nobody loves me." (So now I can start to love myself.)
- "I'm invisible." (But now I can finally see myself.)

- "I'm nobody." (So now I can be who I want to be.)
- "I'll never get it right." (So I'll stop trying and instead explore my heart's desire.)
- "I have failed." (According to an outward definition that no longer suits me.)
- "I can never go home." (Home is where the heart is.)

Do you see how your protagonist's desire has ironically prevented them from achieving their goal?

Until tomorrow,
Al

GROUP DISCUSSION TOPIC FOR TODAY

Does it feel like you're shedding your old skin? Is it uncomfortable? Does it feel like you're in a tunnel with no light at the end? You're not alone. This seems to be a rite of passage, an essential aspect of the journey. This is going to pass soon. Stay with the process. You're heading for a breakthrough.

DAY 77

"Abandon hope, all ye who enter here."
—DANTE'S DIVINE COMEDY

ABANDON HOPE

Dear Writer,

Have you ever seen a dog waiting for their master at a window with their wet nose pressed against the glass, eyes watching the street expectantly for any sign of their beloved guardian? It's sort of sweet, right?

But what if I told you their guardian, let's call him Biff, was never coming home? What if Biff died, or maybe he's on a bender, or he decided to do some traveling and didn't bother sending Thunder to a kennel? Now it's sort of heartbreaking, isn't it?

This is what hope can do.

Hope can keep you waiting for a better situation that's never going to arrive. Hope can make you profess blind loyalty to a lost cause. Hope can prevent you from stepping into your true power.

As long as Thunder believes he's dependent on Biff for his needs, his existence is fraught with panic and dread. He oscillates between relief that Biff might bring home some kibble and anxiety that Biff might never return. Thunder is hungry. Thunder doesn't want to go to the bathroom on the new linoleum but he can't help it — and now he burns with shame that he made a mess. Perhaps he fears he'll be punished and maybe he even believes that he deserves this mistreatment. We all know it isn't Thunder's fault — but tell that to Thunder.

Notice how, in our attempts to get our needs met, we compromise ourselves, accept mistreatment, and sometimes even mistreat others. When we're in survival mode we become disconnected from ourselves. Perhaps we've been living like this for so long that we no longer have a frame of reference for who we truly are.

Do you see how hope can lead to denial? And yet without hope, where would we be? What if Thunder did make a run for it? What if he was a 150-pound Rottweiler and he leapt through the plate glass window and bolted? Now he's got a whole new problem. He's hungry, lonely, and scared, he doesn't know if he can make it out there in the big bad world. And what if his bid for survival caused him to miss Biff's return by just a few minutes?

Do you see the dilemma? Is hope a stepping stone or a dead end? And how do we differentiate? If Thunder leaves, he could perish, but if he stays . . . well, he could also perish — or worse, live out the rest of his days dependent on Biff and his spirit could die!

There comes a point in your life where the pain of staying in a lousy situation becomes greater than the fear of leaving it. And so, Thunder crashes through the window, sending shards everywhere (that bastard Biff never sprang for a doggy door!) and now he's bleeding and hungry and he arrives at this place, some brick walled alley in a bad neighborhood filled with piles of rotting garbage. It's humid, flies are buzzing, his stomach is empty, and he's suddenly aware of how woefully ill equipped he is to engineer his liberation. He wonders if he's made a terrible mistake, but now he can't return because when Biff sees the broken window, that'll be it. Remember, Biff is bad news.

This is Thunder's dark night of the soul.

But then something happens. Someone enters the alley. And what does Thunder do? He bares his teeth. He growls, ready to attack. He could destroy this person in a matter of seconds but then where would he be?

This person reaches out their hand. "Well, hello there," says Sally.

And it is in this moment, that Thunder faces his destiny. He can attack, or he can surrender the fight. (Remember, surrender doesn't mean giving up. It means letting go of our old way of seeing things.)

Do you see how Thunder will never go back to the ways things were? In being *willing* to lose everything, he has choices that were previously unavailable to him. And this is the gift for your protagonist. This is the miracle. Thunder could tear anyone apart if he wanted to. (Don't we all have access to murderous rage as a last resort?) But the larger question, the more difficult question is, "How can I trust, when I have no frame of reference that I can count on anyone?" And the answer is that it comes from within. Thunder's miracle is simply this: he realizes he has a choice. He's willing to trust because he now knows that if it doesn't work out with Sally, he can leave. *By virtue of having nothing to lose, he has stepped into his true power.*

Do you see where this lives in your story? Do you see how your protagonist is beginning to glimpse that there is a different way of seeing themselves and the world? Do you see how your protagonist doesn't even need to leave their situation? They just need to be *willing* to leave, to recognize that they have a choice.

This doesn't mean the choices are great, at least not initially, but simply that there is one and that it can lead to a new way of being. Do you see how, in spite of beginning victimized, your protagonist is no longer defined by their setbacks? Your protagonist is not letting go of their past — that's impossible — they're letting go of the meaning they made out of it.

What if the rest of the world isn't Biff?

It was never Thunder's job to make Biff a capable guardian. It was his job to accept the reality of his situation and leave. This is your protagonist's moment of clarity. And while their situation hasn't changed, they see it in a new way. They are no longer defined by their failure to achieve what was impossible to achieve based on their current approach.

Abandoning hope introduces your protagonist to their true self.

Abandoning hope leads to a new beginning.

Abandoning hope is the start of Act Three.

Until tomorrow,

Al

GROUP DISCUSSION TOPIC FOR TODAY

Have you ever done something that terrified you, and then it turned out to be a positive experience? Did it change the way you see the world? Do you see where this experience lives for your protagonist?

WEEK 12

ACT THREE:
YOUR PROTAGONIST TAKES ACTION

This week your protagonist is going to take action towards giving themselves what they need (as opposed to what they want). Notice how they have found their voice. This is the birth of wisdom, but it doesn't mean that your story is over. Far from it. Notice how your protagonist must confront antagonists on a whole new level as a result of having stepped into their true power.

DAY 78

"I can be changed by what happens to me. But I refuse to be reduced by it."   —MAYA ANGELOU

ACCEPTING REALITY

Dear Writer,

Act Three is about integration. Remember, you have a higher self and a lower self. There's your atavistic survival instinct but there's another side, a spiritual side that hungers for something beyond mere survival, a side that is willing to risk everything in order to experience true freedom.

Do you see how — as the result of your protagonist's dark night of the soul — a gift has appeared? It could be a physical gift or simply a new way of seeing your situation. Have you ever wanted something really badly, a relationship, a job, validation from a parent . . . and it didn't happen? The relationship blew up, the job vanished, you discovered that your parents were simply too limited to see your true self.

This moment can arrive with such existential force that it threatens to shake your foundations — you become dizzy with despair, perhaps even questioning whether or not you can go on living.

And then, the strangest thing happens. You begin to feel the earth under your feet, the gentle breeze on your skin. You listen to the quiet inhale and exhale of your breath. And you suddenly discover that in spite of the fact that life as you know it is over . . .

. . . you're still here.

The world is still walking past your front window, folks are eating ice cream cones, helicopters are buzzing overhead, and the crocuses are blooming on the side of the freeway.

Everything is different now. And yet nothing has changed.

This is the gift (and however you choose to illustrate or dramatize it is up to you and your brilliant imagination). It is the moment you realize that your very existence, just the simple fact of you, is a miracle.

Do you see how you had to be stripped of everything in order to arrive at this profound truth? Unimbued with meaning, it seems like nothing more than a greeting card aphorism. This is the difference between showing and telling. You have taken us on a rocket ship directly into the sun, and you have come out the other side of this crucible, stripped of everything that wasn't you. Newly reborn and you don't know if you're going to be okay or how anything is going to end up. You have no idea if your dream is going to come true but you know something now that you didn't know before.

Life, right here, right now, is precious. All that other stuff that you thought gave your life meaning, including the object of your affection, pales in comparison to this. You are here, and you matter.

This is the beginning of self-love, and there cannot be a Third Act without it.

This gift arrives in the most unexpected form, and if it had come any earlier, you might never have valued it. It's like that moment when you look at your best friend across the table and suddenly realize that the love of your life, the one you've been searching the globe for, is sitting right in front of you.

As Alexander Graham Bell said, "When one door closes, another opens."

What happens to your protagonist as a result of their dark night of the soul? What is the gift that emerges? Do you see how something shifts? A light appears at the end of the tunnel, and you begin to see your situation in a new way.

Until tomorrow,
Al

GROUP DISCUSSION TOPIC FOR TODAY

Are you finding this process liberating? Unnerving? Both? Story involves the *betrayal of a lie*. Do you see the lie that you are betraying, some limiting belief that was passed down to you by your ancestors, something that you simply accepted as true? Notice your disloyalty to this notion? How does it feel?

WEEK 12: THOUGHTS AND REMINDERS

- As a result of surrender, your protagonist accepts the reality of their situation. This moment often heralds a gift. It may be a physical gift, or it may come in the form of an insight.

- Your protagonist often begins to understand the nature of their dilemma at the beginning of Act Three. They begin to see that what they wanted was impossible to achieve based on their current approach.

- Act Three involves your protagonist letting go of what they want so they can pursue what they need.

- When you're struggling with your story, it can be helpful to inquire into the *nature* of your struggle. This is often where your story problem lies. What if your protagonist understood that acceptance did not mean weak resignation, but rather a willingness to accept things as they are?

- The goal of your first draft is simply to get to the end of your story.

HOMEWORK FOR THE WEEK

1. Write a quick point-form outline of Act Three. (Maximum twenty minutes.)
2. Find a point midway through Act Three and write to that point.

DAY 79

*"We don't even know how strong we are until we
are forced to bring that hidden strength forward.
In times of tragedy, of war, of necessity, people do
amazing things. The human capacity for survival
and renewal is awesome."*   **—ISABEL ALLENDE**

COMING OUT OF THE DEEP FREEZE (REBIRTH)

Dear Writer,

Frostbite is only painful when your fingers begin to thaw. In Act
Three your protagonist begins to thaw, and this can cause pain. But
it is the exquisite pain of coming to life — it is the cry of the child as
they emerge from the birth canal, the wail of the spouse at the loss
of their partner, the whoop of the diver as they emerge from the icy
depths. The beginning of Act Three involves the pain of resurrection.
This is where your protagonist has connected to their truth. They
have tapped into a new reason to live. There's something that
they're willing to die for because they've connected to something
within them that transcends their ego or their physical self. Notice,
as your protagonist speaks their truth, that they are confronting
your antagonists in an entirely different way.

Now let's do an exercise. Make a list of three antagonists in
your story. For example:

ANTAGONISTS

Bill – husband

Sally – best friend

Kate – Bill's ex-wife

Write for two minutes on your protagonist's relationship to each one of these characters. Notice what images and ideas emerge.

It's important to remember that an antagonist is not a *bad guy*. Story isn't about good and bad or right and wrong. Story is about cause and effect, action and consequence. Story is about universal law — and you are not playing God. Remember, you're not the author, you're the channel, and your characters are three-dimensional. Nobody is all good or all bad.

Notice how your protagonist, as a direct result of their surrender, is relating differently to these characters at this point in your story.

Until tomorrow,

Al

GROUP DISCUSSION TOPIC FOR TODAY

Can you identify a moment in your own life where suddenly a gift appeared from the most unexpected place?

DAY 80

*"The higher we soar, the smaller we appear to those
who cannot fly."*   —FRIEDRICH NIETZSCHE

FREEDOM

Dear Writer,

When your protagonist accepts the reality of their situation, they begin to move in the direction of giving themselves what they need as opposed to what they want. This doesn't mean they've given up what they want, but they recognize now that if they don't give themselves what they need, they will forever be in bondage to their outward desire.

Notice where your protagonist's priorities are shifting at this point. Perhaps they are considering themselves in ways that they had not allowed themselves to do previously.

Notice that the messages they unconsciously accepted as truths are now bubbling to the surface of their consciousness, such as: *If you don't put others first, it means you're selfish. You won't survive without your beloved. You are weak. You are lazy. You are too tall, too short, too fat, too skinny, too dark, too light, too loud, too abrasive, too shy. You're not smart enough, or beautiful enough, or rich enough, or (fill in the blank) enough . . . to have your heart's desire.*

This growing awareness creates all sorts of new challenges for your protagonist. Notice how it is leading your protagonist to relate differently to all of the antagonists in your story. Do you see how the stakes are rising as the antagonists in their life are met with this newly awakened person? Do you see how it is leading to conflict? (Don't confuse conflict with hostility, by the way. Conflict can simply mean that there is tension as your protagonist attempts to navigate the world from this new place.) Notice how, when one person starts to shift or change, the entire system starts to change.

Have you ever noticed that when you decided to make a major change in your life, the universe seemed to test you? This is what is happening for your protagonist at this point. The good news, however, is that your protagonist no longer has anything to lose. They're no longer willing to back down from a confrontation, no longer willing to put off their dreams, no longer willing to postpone their grief.

Your protagonist is no longer willing to remain stuck. This might sound obvious, but there are subtle payoffs one gets from staying stuck, and while being stuck might be unpleasant, at least it is familiar. Remember, human beings don't like change. Are you noticing the new approach your protagonist has adopted, and how this is moving them towards the possibility of greater freedom? But freedom comes at a price. It involves dropping the old story we've been telling ourselves.

- The cost of freedom may mean no longer identifying as a victim.
- The cost of success may mean no longer seeing oneself as a loser.
- The cost of wisdom may mean saying goodbye to one's innocence.
- The cost of wisdom may mean closing the door on blind faith.
- The cost of love may mean letting go of fear.

Until tomorrow,
Al

GROUP DISCUSSION TOPIC FOR TODAY

We're in Act 3. Are you experiencing your protagonist in a new way? Are they finding their voice? Speaking their truth? Does their truth surprise you?

DAY 81

"To err is human, to forgive divine."
—**Alexander Pope**

FORGIVENESS

Dear Writer,

Story is about the undoing of a pattern. Oftentimes, the pain your protagonist has endured is due to their misguided attempts to get what they want, which leads to a host of poor decisions they repeat until arriving at a place of surrender. Ironically, it is your protagonist's unwillingness to forgive themselves that keeps them stuck in this pattern.

As you move into Act Three, you may notice that the question of forgiveness arises. The stakes are rising, the tension is mounting, and while the dilemma has become apparent to your protagonist, it is far from being resolved. Act Three is where your protagonist takes action towards giving themselves what they need as opposed to what they want. And as they do this, they continue to press against their dilemma.

In Act One and Act Two, your protagonist may only glimpse two options: fight or give up. In Act Three, as a result of their dark night of the soul, a third option as emerged: take the risk of losing everything you value and step into your true power.

The beginning of Act Three involves the betrayal of a lie but the lie that your protagonist is betraying is a false belief that's been passed down to them by their ancestors. It could be that love must be earned, or that they are destined to fail, or that they will always be alone. Act Three is where the true work of forgiveness begins but what is being forgiven is not the action but rather the *meaning* your protagonist has made out of the action. In other words, their false belief is coming up for review.

As Reinhold Niebuhr, the author of the Serenity Prayer said, *"Forgiveness is the final form of love."* I believe that the love Niebuhr is referring to is self-love. The irony is that this newfound self-love often elicits greater conflict, at least, temporarily. Perhaps your protagonist is willing to stand up for themselves —no longer willing to be taken advantage of — and this may lead to confrontation. Or they may recognize their complicity in a drama that finally leads them to make amends, which is another form of self-forgiveness.

Forgiveness rises out of compassion for oneself. In conflict, anger is often a quick and easy tool to reach for. While it may give us a temporary sense of power and control, the conflict often escalates, creating a cycle of shame that leads to an ongoing attempt for your protagonist to outrun a deep-rooted sense of their fundamental unworthiness. Your protagonist may have the mistaken notion that if they endure enough abuse it will make up for the harms they caused, and this can create a pattern of self-abuse that continues indefinitely until they break the cycle by separating the action from the intention. The action that led to shame and self-recrimination was a function of their desire to temporarily comfort themselves. Yes, your protagonist must take responsibility, but this doesn't mean your protagonist is conscripted to a life of self-recrimination. The true crime was the low self-worth that led to the action.

Act Three arrives as an opportunity for your protagonist to correct their outward approach to life by accepting the reality of their situation and responding in a way that liberates them. Simply letting someone off the hook, without installing new boundaries or understanding the nature of the offense, is not forgiveness — it's denial. Act Three is where your protagonist finally recognizes that they've been carrying someone else's pain and they become willing to hand it back.

Let's say, for example, that your protagonist is struggling with the complicated grief of a parent's suicide. How does forgiveness figure into this? Perhaps they're struggling with the dilemma of yearning for someone who is never coming back while also carrying rage (whether consciously or not) for this abandonment. There's an internal war going on inside of them between their yearning and their fury, creating an unrelenting stream of anguish and guilt that never seems to subside. Perhaps they wonder if they had been better behaved then this might never have happened. The guilt and confusion can manifest in chronic depression that persists for decades. Perhaps the protagonist goes to therapy and talks about it endlessly, but it never seems to go away.

This is because the goal of making it go away is the very thing that is prolonging the despair. Oftentimes, the despair itself becomes a comfort, a way of trying to hold onto the dead parent. The notion that it is possible to make the pain go away is the false belief. The irony is that when the protagonist begins to allow themselves to experience the pain, it begins a long-delayed grieving process as the dilemma starts to resolve itself, thus leading to a lessening of the pain.

Once the dilemma is resolved, one can actually grieve the loss and let them go. Does this mean there isn't sadness? Of course not. But now the situation has become workable. And now your protagonist is moving into action.

Until tomorrow,
Al

GROUP DISCUSSION TOPIC FOR TODAY

Is your protagonist changing? Are they standing up for themselves? Are they more vulnerable? Are they more willing to walk through fear? What are you noticing?

DAY 82

"Do you want to know who you are? Don't ask. Act!
Action will delineate and define you."
—**WITOLD GOMBROWICZ**

TAKING ACTION

Dear Writer,

Your protagonist is taking action now. Your protagonist is not afraid of confrontation or at least they aren't letting that prevent them from speaking their truth.

Notice at this stage in your story how your protagonist may experience suffering, but it is a different kind of suffering. They are no longer willing to be taken advantage of. They have connected to their truth. There's something that they are willing to die for because they have connected to something within themselves that transcends their ego or their physical self.

In Act Three, your protagonist takes action toward giving themselves what they need (as opposed to what they want). This doesn't mean that they don't still want what they want but that they now realize the fact that until they satisfy their inner need, they will forever be in bondage to their outward desire.

It is important to notice how your protagonist is always taking action. As writers we tend to be passive observers and there can be a tendency, particularly in memoir, to have a reactive protagonist — one who merely responds to events.

You might say, "But that is what happened," and I would submit that that is only what *appeared* to happen. Remember that we are always making choices in response to external forces. While staying in a lousy marriage may appear passive, it is also a daily choice. The challenge lies in dramatizing the "staying." Why does the character stay? What is the dilemma besetting them? We will not understand why the character is staying except through some kind of action. Let's say their spouse comes home drunk and is abusive, and the protagonist threatens to leave, and the drunk says that if they leave they will never see their child again. Dilemma. The action for the protagonist is the threat. Without the threat of leaving, there is no context for why they stay.

Don't confuse inertia with passivity. Outwardly, Hamlet appears passive but inwardly he is constantly plotting and scheming. Don't confuse the inner experience with the external behavior. As storytellers, we must dramatize; meaning is conveyed through action.

For example, let's say I tell a story about my piano teacher who repeatedly told me that I had no talent and I remained silent each time he insulted me. While there seems to be little action externally, how can I dramatize the internal shifts? Perhaps the first time he insults me, I might choose to believe him and deny the rage I'm feeling, *burying it in shame.* The second time I might *congratulate myself for my improvement* despite his cruelty, and the next time I might leave and find a teacher who supports me in learning this new skill. So, although I appeared passive, the meaning shifted with each insult, which finally led to a new behavior. In other words, your choices indicate your characters' wants or desires, and that provides your story with meaning.

Make your protagonist active, at least internally, so we understand what is driving them.

Until tomorrow,
Al

GROUP DISCUSSION TOPIC FOR TODAY

You're almost there. What are you feeling? Sometimes we can feel a heaviness. That's grief. You're grieving the loss of your old self as you move toward transformation. Can you make some space for yourself today to allow these feelings to move through you?

DAY 83

"I have learnt through bitter experience the one supreme lesson, to conserve my anger, and as heat conserved is transmuted into energy, even so our anger controlled can be transmuted into a power which can move the world."

—**MAHATMA GANDHI**

THE CRUCIBLE

Dear Writer,

As the result of your protagonist's dark night of the soul, they emerge from this crucible forever changed. They see their situation in a new way.

When we have nothing to lose, we don't burn up energy concerning ourselves with what others think of us. We don't waste time bothering with things beyond our control. Our focus gets clarified. We summon the angels and we move in the direction of our truth.

I used to run track in high school and one of my heroes was Dave Wottle. He ran the 800 meters in the 1972 Munich Olympics. After the first lap he was running dead last. There were seven runners in front of him, and the gap between himself and the second last runner was shockingly, embarrassingly wide. If you watch the race on YouTube you'll hear the commentator actually suggest that Dave's perhaps been injured. In fact, he doesn't even fit in the wide shot of the runners, he's so incredibly far behind — and just for context, the 800 is practically a sprint. It lasts a little over a minute and a half.

Dave Wottle later explained to an interviewer, "I wasn't thinking about winning. I just didn't want to embarrass my country by coming in last." And so, he sets his sights on runner number seven, and gradually he pulls up alongside him and passes him. And then, he trains his focus on runner number six. Passes him. And then, it's runner number five . . .

. . . you see where this is going.

It is one of the most astonishing feats in the history of track and field and a true testament to showing up and letting go of the results. As Wottle comes into the final lap and moves to the outside, he gradually inches past runner number three, and finally, heading into the straightaway, he starts his sprint and passes number two and now, in second place, with the finish line merely yards away, he drives harder, reaching deeper than he maybe ever has before. With millimeters to spare, Wottle passes the leader and wins the gold medal by a single hundredth of a second. It is truly breath-taking, and even though I've watched this race at least fifty times, each time I'm still shocked when he wins.

Notice how your protagonist is no longer willing to sell out, to give up, or to submit to something they know isn't true. It isn't important for your protagonist to win. And while that may have been their goal in the beginning, to achieve some kind of victory, to find some kind of answer that would lead to some idea of freedom or happiness, their only goal now is to be most fully who they were meant to be.

Keep on going. Keep on trusting yourself.

Until tomorrow,
Al

GROUP DISCUSSION TOPIC FOR TODAY

How are your antagonists responding to this new person? Do you see how the stakes are continuing to rise?

DAY 84

"All the really exciting things possible during the course of a lifetime require a little more courage than we currently have. A deep breath and a leap."
—JOHN PATRICK SHANLEY

FRESH COURAGE

Dear Writer,

As the result of your protagonist's surrender, something starts to happen. While their outward circumstance has not changed, it has been reframed. What seemed hopeless suddenly becomes workable.

Notice how that cry into the void has taken on new meaning. Where "all is lost" originally meant despair, it now invites a fresh start. Your protagonist can shed everything that was keeping them tied to their past and they can move forward from a place of truth. They don't know if they will ever be free, but they do know that they can never go back to the way things were.

Let's be clear — the obstacles are not going away but they no longer look the same as they did last week or last year.

Your protagonist no longer has anything to lose.

Until tomorrow,
Al

GROUP DISCUSSION TOPIC FOR TODAY

Did something just happen in your story that you weren't expecting? Is it possible that a perceived enemy became an ally? Are you beginning to see how they can no longer hurt you since you took your power back? Are you open to the surprises that are arising?

THE ENDING

ACT THREE:
YOUR PROTAGONIST RETURNS HOME

This week your protagonist is going to fight a battle. This is an internal battle between what they want and what they need, though you may want to find a way to dramatize it externally through a difficult choice. This new choice heralds your protagonist's return home.

DAY 85

"No one is free until we are all free."
    —MARTIN LUTHER KING, JR.

WE ARE ALL CONNECTED

Dear Writer,

It is human nature to search for absolutes. Joe is a liar, while Helen is trustworthy. Abe is punctual while Ruth is always late. Absolutes give us the illusion of security but they also lead to lazy stories because they simply aren't true. When we employ absolutes, we are trading in generalities, and that leads to cliché.

It is the curious writer that scratches the surface of their characters' actions to investigate the impulses that informed them. And it is the brave and empathic writer who investigates where those impulses live within themselves, because this provides their characters with true humanity. If we don't do this, we may miss the true lesson that our story is offering us.

There's a certain distance that gets created when we write off a character's actions as anomalous — it lacks curiosity. If you want to write a compelling conclusion to your memoir, you must explore a true resolution that doesn't wrap your story up into a neat bow. In memoir, a tidy conclusion is rarely a satisfying one.

For example, while it may be obvious to say that a drug czar's actions are heinous and evil, it is also reductive. What is far more frightening to consider is how he's able to persuade thousands of others to do his bidding. We hear stories of the Mexican drug cartels who take men living in poverty and force them to commit violence in order to survive. While these men are perpetrators, they are also victims. It is the same, perhaps, for some of the Mexican police who fear they cannot afford to take care of their families and so they accept bribes. There are customs agents and politicians who are on the grift. And what about the otherwise law-abiding citizens who purchase the narcotics? While they may not be guilty of murder, without their financial involvement, the violence may likely not have occurred.

There is a cause and effect, a ripple that travels throughout the world that connects us all to each other. By examining the circumstances of your characters and exploring their backstories, you will begin to understand their motives and perhaps gain greater compassion for them. As human beings, we are all connected and therefore, on some level — on some level — we are also complicit. This is not to say that we are, each of us, responsible for the drug trade — of course not — but until we recognize that we are all connected, we tend to judge the actions of others without being curious about the circumstances that drove them. Until we empathize with the circumstances, we will fail to see our story as clearly as possible.

When your protagonist focuses solely on freeing themselves, notice how they move further into bondage. When their focus is on happiness, notice how it leads to misery. But when their focus shifts outward toward connection to others, notice how, ironically, they become compassionate, forgiving, and thus move in the direction of fulfilling their inner need.

Until tomorrow,
Al

GROUP DISCUSSION TOPIC FOR TODAY

Do you realize what a magnificent gift you are to the world? Whether you do or not, this is the truth. When you peel away all of your defenses, you are left with pure magic, your fundamental self. Can you sit with that? Do you see where it lives for your protagonist?

YOUR PROTAGONIST RETURNS HOME: THOUGHTS AND REMINDERS

- Your protagonist's dilemma is resolved during the battle scene.

- Your protagonist's want and need collide in the battle scene. Despite what they want, they choose what they need, thus proving to the gods they have earned their transformation.

- The battle scene involves a choice for your protagonist. Make it active.

- "Active" does not necessarily mean "external." It can be an internal shift but you must find a way to dramatize it so that your reader can experience it. In other words, it's not enough to say that your protagonist lived happily ever after. We must experience what that means.

- The battle scene is just that, a battle. It is a difficult choice. If it was easy, your protagonist would have made the choice in Act One.

- A satisfying ending to a story is a total surprise and yet it is utterly inevitable. It could not have ended any other way. The seed of the ending was planted in the beginning.

- What does your protagonist come to understand as the result of their journey?

- Notice how your ending is bittersweet. Freedom comes at a price. The cost of wisdom is innocence. The cost of growing up is the death of our youth.

- • In the end, your protagonist is returned home. What does this new equilibrium look like?

HOMEWORK

1. Write a quick point-form outline to the end of your novel. (Twenty minutes maximum.)
2. Write to the end of the first draft of your novel.

DAY 86

*"You cannot swim for new horizons until you have
courage to lose sight of the shore."*
—WILLIAM FAULKNER

TAKING THE RISK TO LOVE

Dear Writer,

I've been with my wife Mary-Beth since 2005, and married since 2007. She's the kindest, wisest, most compassionate person I know. Marrying her was the best decision I ever made, and yet . . .

I don't have words to express how terrifying it was for me to get married. Intimacy does not come naturally for me. Something I've discovered about myself over the years is that it is easy for me to feel love for others, for my wife and son, for my students. When I work with writers and artists, the doors of my heart seem to effortlessly swing open, and yet . . .

Why does it feel scary for me to let love in? I'm aware of how much my family loves me and I frequently hear gratitude and even love from my students, and it moves me. Then, for some strange reason, it becomes almost painful. (Actually, it used to — it doesn't anymore.) I used to brush off compliments or make self-deprecating remarks until I realized it was diminishing to the person paying the compliment.

Do you see a moment in your story where you recognize the need to open your heart, to let love in, despite the risk? It could be a moment where you realize that to love means to be willing to lose, to risk being abandoned or even betrayed. It might also be a moment when to truly love means to finally put yourself first. Perhaps your protagonist is waking up to the fact that they have been giving themselves away or being taken advantage of for far too long. Taking the risk to love can come in many forms. It doesn't need to be romantic — it can be familial, a friendship, or even a work situation.

Notice the moment where your protagonist recognizes the cost of not opening their heart and living from their truth. This noticing is often a gradual process, an unfolding. But as your protagonist moves towards the end of the story, notice where this risk is demanding to be taken.

Until tomorrow,
Al

GROUP DISCUSSION TOPIC FOR TODAY

Do you see how your protagonist has grown or changed from the beginning? Are you surprised by this change? Are you holding onto an idea that such a change is impossible? Are you sure it is impossible? Remember, story traces the journey of the impossible. What if you gave yourself permission to imagine true freedom for your protagonist? What does that look like?

DAY 87

"Only the self-deceived will claim perfect freedom from fear."   —BILL WILSON

THE BATTLE SCENE: THERE IS NO CLOSURE

Dear Writer,

There is no such thing as a tidy ending, a happily ever after, or a rapturous denouement that doesn't arrive at great expense. It is important to understand that transformation does not mean one is liberated from the vicissitudes of life. We will still struggle. We will still suffer. We will still fail. However . . .

. . . there's a reason you're telling this story. There is something you're going to understand at the end of your story that you didn't understand at the beginning. There's something that wants to be expressed through these series of events that leads you to some greater understanding of yourself and the world.

In the end, we understand something about the nature of your struggle that we didn't understand at the beginning. And while the ache of your suffering may never fully vanish, it can get reframed into something that is workable. Perhaps there's a way to make meaning out of your suffering so your experience can be of benefit to others.

Your story is likely about integrating your pain, recognizing what belongs to you and what doesn't. You may be glimpsing that the shame or limiting beliefs you carried were never yours to begin with, that they are inherited wounds passed down to you by your ancestors. You may also notice that none of this was done consciously, therefore none of it was personal. That doesn't make it any less dangerous, any less urgent, or any less real, but it does make it workable.

I tell my writers your protagonist's *desire* prevents them from achieving their *goal*. Consider this: if your desire to be free is preventing you from true freedom, or your desire for security is standing in the way of your experiencing real security, then how on earth can you ever achieve your goal?

By letting go of the *meaning* you make out of your goal. By making a new choice.

As long as I believe that marrying Sue will make me happy, or that working at a bank will finally win my father's approval, or that curing cancer will make me a success, I will forever be in bondage to external forces to solve an inward dilemma.

The answer lies not in attempting to get what you want, but in making peace with the possibility that your dream might never come true . . . and that's okay. But here's the kicker: Your dream was simply an *idea*, a fantasy of how things should go — it was merely another form of control. When you let it go, the universe opens up to give you your heart's desire which is often something beyond your imagination.

Notice how your protagonist is resisting this universal law. *This is the battle scene of your story.* This is where your protagonist must make a difficult choice between what they *want* and what they *need*.

But here's the amazing thing. In letting go, it becomes possible to have it . . . but only if it belongs in your life. By letting go of control, it becomes possible to have a reality beyond your wildest dreams. It just may look unlike anything you imagined.

Do you see where this moment lives in your story?

Notice how your desire for closure, for a solid answer, for a tidy wrap up, may be standing between you and your most powerful ending.

Trust the truth.

When you let go of your desire for an intellectual understanding of your ending, you make room for an ending that moves you beyond your preconceived idea of where things should go.

Perhaps closure is not actually what you're seeking. Perhaps what you're seeking is the opposite — an opening. What does it look like when your heart opens? What does it look like when you discover that your heart can break a million times but that it just keeps breaking open? What does it look like when you discover that within you is something indestructible — that all of your ideas of how things should go are the very thing standing between you and true liberation?

Until tomorrow,
Al

GROUP DISCUSSION TOPIC FOR TODAY

Love is a choice. How and who are you choosing to love today? Are you doing it out of guilt? Do you have boundaries and discernment? Do you see where this lives for your protagonist in your story?

DAY 88

"If you do not tell the truth about yourself, you cannot tell it about other people." —**VIRGINIA WOOLF**

EMBRACE THE ORDINARY

Dear Writer,

When my son was a toddler, he sat at the table eating his breakfast and while chewing his food, he would stare up at me unblinking, like he was gazing into my soul. It was sublime, simultaneously thrilling and unnerving. In those moments, I didn't quite know who I was, if he had the answer or if I did — if I was his father or if in some weird way he was mine. I wondered if I was supposed to impart some great wisdom as I stared back into his dark chestnut eyes. Gazing at him filled me with awe but also dread. It felt like my soul was on trial and I feared what dark secrets he might uncover. I was filled with a deep sense of responsibility, that I somehow knew I could never quite live up to but I had to try.

In plot terms, these moments were uneventful, utterly ordinary in that nothing outwardly was happening; we weren't climbing Everest or trekking the Iditarod or trapped deep in a well. I mean, what could be more ordinary than two humans gazing into each other's eyes? But they were moments I will never forget. My son was so vulnerable, so innocent, and he was unwittingly inviting me to join him in what is probably the bravest thing we can do: to be truly present and emotionally naked with another human being.

Your extraordinariness lies in your willingness to be ordinary, to shed all your pretense, all the striving and questing you think will make you more acceptable. Do you understand that you were acceptable from the beginning?

Can you own this? Can you dramatize it — put it into action?

Remember you're not the author, you're the channel, and when you trust your ordinariness, your truth naturally emerges. You begin to see clearly because your sight is no longer clouded with apprehension or hope. The strangest thing begins to happen. You begin to see that while the facts of your situation may not have changed much, your relationship to them is quite different.

Until tomorrow,
Al

GROUP DISCUSSION TOPIC FOR TODAY

Is it okay to not have answers today? Is it okay to lose yourself in the truth of your characters' experiences, without knowing exactly how your story will end?

DAY 89

"Deserve your dream."   —OCTAVIO PAZ

COMING HOME

Dear Writer,

The desire to write is really the desire to evolve by resolving an inner struggle. While your creative work is a gift to yourself and the world, it is also simply a byproduct of your spiritual growth.

Something powerful happens when you write down your thoughts and experiences. They are made fully conscious. It is different than an oral recitation. They are made real — a witness statement, a public reclaiming of your truest self.

Your protagonist began their journey way back there. It was like they were in a cocoon and while it may not have been comfortable, it was certainly familiar. But then something happened and they were forced to respond and this awakened in them a dilemma. "Do I stay here in the familiar or do I risk all that I know and venture out into the unknown?"

They weighed their options only to realize that their heart was calling them to go on a quest. While this may have elicited feelings of guilt or betrayal, it also was quite thrilling, and deep down they knew that if they stayed here in this place, they would surely wither and die. And so they set out on their journey and they soon discovered that there was a world out there that was much larger than they'd imagined. It was exotic and seductive, and there were so many choices and opportunities. They were overcome, however briefly, with the sense that victory was within their grasp. They swelled with hope and optimism that they could conquer or vanquish their foe.

But then something happened. They discovered that they were being tested. This new world had worthy antagonists — in fact, on some level, these antagonists had a strange resemblance to where they came from, and the struggle that they were running from seemed to follow them and was now manifesting itself in new and more sophisticated ways.

But they knew in their bones that they could never return to where they had come from, and so they redoubled their efforts and this led to suffering. They may even have wished that they had never set out on this journey. Perhaps they would have been better off remaining in that little cocoon? But that option is over and thus they wander the desert in search of sustenance. Everything is a mirage, a pale reflection of the thing their heart is seeking. Nothing looks like what they had hoped it would. And suddenly, they find themselves at this place of despair. Despite all their efforts, they have come to the devastating realization that nothing out there can ever fulfill their inner yearning. They are lost and alone and too far from home.

They squeeze their eyes shut and fall to their knees. They cry out to their mother. They want nothing now except to know that they are not alone. And as they open their eyes, the faintest glimmer of light glows like a beacon in the distance.

They pull themselves up and stagger forward, no longer carried by hope but by something else, a curiosity that transcends their battle-weary self. They are no longer burdened by their ego and all of their competing and conflicting emotions. They have shed that part of their self that believed they could conquer anything or even that they were supposed to. Their energy is contained now and focused solely on that light in the distance. The antagonists have not retreated but now something really weird has happened — your protagonist's unwillingness to battle with them has transformed some of them into allies.

Your protagonist has let go of everything they thought gave their life value, and they have discovered something within themselves — an indestructible truth, a place at the core of their being that can never be bought or traded or sold. It is their true magnificence, a place within them that transcends all their human limitations. They sense that they are connected to the universe in a fundamental way, that they are stardust, and thus indestructible. They are equal to all others. In fact, even the concept of equality seems ridiculous, an intellectual construct — as if we should bother to debate whether or not a stone is equal to a flower.

They see the truth of the universe — they understand their place in it, and they face their final challenge. They are forced to make a difficult choice between what they thought they wanted, and what they truly need, and while this test may be difficult, and one that they would surely have failed at the beginning of their journey, they now know in their heart what must be done. And so they choose, thereby proving to the gods that they have earned their transformation. And ironically, the moment the choice is made, it instantly becomes the most obvious thing in the world.

And in doing so, they are returned home. They have been stripped of all their defenses. They have laid down their weapons of dishonesty and self-pity, and they have entered the circle, a humble warrior revered and respected for their inner strength and wisdom. They are connected to a tribe of brave and creative beings whose only weapon is their pen, and with it their ability to pierce the hearts and minds of the world.

Until tomorrow,
Al

GROUP DISCUSSION TOPIC FOR TODAY

What are you noticing today? Check in with yourself and let your group know what you are feeling.

DAY 90

"Today you are You, that is truer than true. There is no one alive who is You-er than You!"—DR. SEUSS

CELEBRATE

Dear Writer,

There's an apocryphal story of Lao Tzu, the author of the *Tao Te Ching*. He was considered a holy man and one day, having grown weary of the moral decay of life in Chengzhou, he decided to leave and spend his remaining days in quiet seclusion. But as he approached the western gates of the village, a guard named Yinxi asked him to record his wisdom.

And so he obliged. He wrote the *Tao Te Ching* and then apparently retired to some cave. Nobody knows who Lao Tzu was. There are no pictures of him, no document of his likeness. But that's not important.

What matters is the message he left.

Your memoir is a living document that describes your journey to the truth. As a result of writing your story, notice how you understand your situation in a new way. Maybe your account was a journey out of victimhood, or perhaps you reframed your relationship to success and discovered that only you can define it, and that it comes from within.

Yes, this was your first draft. It is rough and ragged. There are most likely holes in the narrative. Probably it is incoherent in places. Good! Fantastic! That is the job of the first draft. You did it. You got to the end.

And now, it is time to celebrate!

This is an important aspect of the journey, and not something to dismiss. It is easy to take your subconscious for granted, but as artists we must treat it with reverence. You have accomplished a great thing and now you must make a plan to do something special for yourself.

Take yourself out for a nice meal. Go on a hike. Dance. Scream. Splurge on some really nice cashmere socks. This is a way of honoring yourself and your work. And when you do this, the channel widens, and it makes room for more work. Your subconscious is the seat of your genius. Thank it for its good work.

Go celebrate!

Your fellow writer,
Al

GROUP DISCUSSION TOPIC FOR TODAY

You did it! You're here. Welcome! I'm so thrilled for you. Do you feel different? Lighter? Freer? Emptied out? Do you feel shaky, unsure of what to make of this new person you've become? Share these experiences with your group.

And what are you going to do today to celebrate?

writing exercises

STREAM-OF-CONSCIOUSNESS WRITING EXERCISES

These writing prompts are meant to spark your memory and stimulate your imagination. As you write stream of consciousness for five minutes on any of these questions, a sense of the world of your story will begin to emerge. After a short while, whether it is a few days or a week, begin to incorporate the structure questions into this work of imagining the world of your story. The structure questions invite up images at various stages in your protagonist's journey. By working with them, they will help you deepen your relationship to your story.

From the perspective of your protagonist or an antagonist, write for five minutes on each of the following prompts, beginning with:

1) One thing you still need to know about me is . . .
2) The lie I continually tell myself is . . .
3) What makes me angry is . . .
4) What breaks my heart is . . .
5) The secret I won't tell anyone is . . .
6) The secret I won't tell myself is . . .
7) My perfect day would be . . .
8) This is how I would spend my last day on earth . . .
9) The biggest shock of my life was when . . .
10) I feel trapped when . . .
11) My first love was . . .
12) My biggest regret is . . .
13) My greatest accomplishment has been . . .
14) My childhood dream was . . .
15) When I look in the mirror, I see . . .
16) If you knew me before, you would have said . . .

17) Tomorrow I am going to . . .

18) On my tombstone, it will read . . .

19) What I have come to understand is . . .

20) On my tombstone, I would *like* it to read . . .

21) I fear that when people look at me they see . . .

22) The person I hate the most is . . .

23) You would never know this by looking at me, but . . .

24) My secret love is . . .

25) I can't wait for . . .

26) My attitude toward sex is . . .

27) My philosophy on life is . . .

28) I believe my role in life is to . . .

29) My favorite thing to do is . . .

30) The thought that keeps me up at night is . . .

31) One day I am going to . . .

32) I feel free when . . .

33) The best thing I ever purchased was . . .

34) My favorite memory is . . .

35) My worst memory is . . .

36) When I want to comfort myself, I remember . . .

37) The closest I ever came to murder was when . . .

38) The place I go when I don't want anyone to find me is . . .

39) If you were to ask the closest person in my life who I am, they would say . . .

40) I would be crushed if anyone knew this about me . . .

41) The one thing I care most about is . . .

42) I used to believe that . . .

43) The truth I am resisting about myself is . . .

44) Every time I think I'm going to get what I want, it seems that . . .

45) When I wake up my first thought is . . .

46) My last thought before I fall asleep is . . .

47) I have a habit of . . .

48) The answer to my problem that I've been avoiding is . . .

49) My worst defeat was when . . .

50) I will finally rest when . . .

51) The bravest thing I've ever done is . . .

52) The most cowardly thing I've ever done is . . .

53) My relationship to God is . . .

54) The defining moment of my life was when . . .

55) The greatest love of my life is . . .

56) The last time I remember laughing hard was when . . .

57) The one thing I could never survive is . . .

58) The greatest thrill of my life was when . . .

59) My most painful memory is . . .

60) I need to be forgiven for . . .

61) If I could do one thing differently
    from my past, it would be . . .

62) The message I got from my father was . . .

63) The message I got from my mother was . . .

64) The reason I'm in this situation is because . . .

65) If I were to tell the truth, the consequence would be . . .

66) I believe that . . . (as your protagonist at beginning of story)

67) I know it to be true that . . .
    (as your protagonist at end of story)

68) To me, freedom looks like . . .

69) Something I expect from others is . . .

70) Something I expect from myself is . . .

71) I am terrified of . . .

72) I will never declare defeat when it comes to . . .

73) The bravest person I know is . . .

74) The most cowardly person I know is . . .

75) The smartest thing I ever did was . . .

76) My attitude toward money is . . .

77) My attitude toward work is . . .

78) My attitude toward alcohol is . . .

79) My attitude toward marriage is . . .

80) My attitude toward love is . . .

81)   My attitude toward the opposite sex is . . .

82)   My attitude toward children is . . .

83)   My attitude toward organized religions is . . .

84)   I will die before I . . .

85)   If I had no fear, I would immediately . . .

86)   I will never forget the time that I . . .

87)   I could never live in a world where . . .

88)   The most dangerous thing I've ever done is . . .

89)   The biggest risk I've ever taken is . . .

90)   The most uncomfortable thing I've ever revealed is . . .

91)   I secretly despise . . .

92)   I secretly lust after . . .

93)   I am most ashamed of . . .

94)   I am most disappointed by . . .

95)   I couldn't live without . . .

96)   I resent . . .

97)   I am most envious of . . .

98)   I feel safest when . . .

99)   I am tired of pretending that I like . . .

100) I wouldn't be upset if . . .

101) I shouldn't feel this way, but . . .

102) The most valuable thing I ever stole was . . .

103) The worst crime I ever committed was . . .

104) My most rebellious act was when I . . .

105) Something I did once but will never do again is . . .

106) Something I've always wanted to say
      but don't feel I'm allowed is . . .

107) I have trouble reasoning with . . .

108) I feel lost when . . .

109) I have unrealistic expectations of . . .

110) I am far too understanding of . . .

111) I refuse to believe that . . .

112) Before I die, I am determined to . . .

113) I am appalled by . . .

114) It's been far too long since I . . .
115) I feel intense loyalty towards . . .
116) I know this isn't logical, but . . .
117) I feel misunderstood about . . .
118) A debt that I can never repay is . . .
119) The nicest thing anyone ever said to me was . . .
120) The meanest thing anyone ever said to me was . . .
121) My earliest memory is . . .
122) The last time I cried was when . . .
123) I don't actually remember this, but I'm told that . . .
124) I would describe myself as . . .
125) The person who understands me best is . . .
126) The most intimate moment of my life was when . . .
127) I'm always shocked to hear that . . .
128) The last time I drank too much I . . .
129) The family member I am closest to is . . .
130) Something that I wouldn't trade for the world is . . .
131) A time that I was too trusting was . . .
132) A time that I was too suspicious or cynical was . . .
133) I have difficulty pretending that . . .
134) Something I tend to avoid is . . .
135) My worst habit is . . .
136) What annoys me most about people is . . .
137) What people find most annoying about me is . . .
138) I felt the deepest sense of belonging when . . .
139) The most alienating moment of my life was when . . .
140) The last time I betrayed someone was when I . . .
141) The last time I saved someone was when I . . .
142) The last time I betrayed myself was when I . . .
143) My family wishes that I would . . .
144) Something I regret losing is . . .
145) Something that I regret finding is . . .
146) Something I'm grateful to have lost is . . .
147) Something I'm grateful to have found is . . .

148) I am envious of . . .

149) I feel pity for . . .

150) Something I wish I could forget is . . .

151) When I die, I hope that . . .

152) The most interesting person I've ever known is . . .

153) The most attractive person I've ever known is . . .

154) I wish I were more . . .

155) I can't forgive myself for . . .

156) I'm too hard on myself because . . .

157) I will be redeemed when . . .

158) I will have won when . . .

159) I don't consider myself a selfish person, but . . .

160) I don't consider myself an overly generous person, but . . .

161) I need to apologize for . . .

162) What bores me is . . .

163) What excites me is . . .

164) What lifts my spirits is . . .

165) The last trip I took was . . .

166) What disturbs me is . . .

167) I no longer agree that . . .

168) The purpose of life is to . . .

169) Love is . . .

170) The biggest misperception people have of me is . . .

171) Everything will make sense when . . .

172) I prefer when things are . . .

173) I cannot tolerate . . .

174) I insist upon . . .

175) The most embarrassing thing I ever said was . . .

176) The most embarrassing thing I ever did was . . .

177) The most brilliant thing I ever said was . . .

178) The most brilliant thing I ever did was . . .

179) I live for . . .

180) My life would be over if . . .

181) My greatest hope is . . .

182) My best quality is . . .

183) Let me tell you how I feel about my physical appearance . . .

184) I believe that love can . . .

185) I don't believe that love can . . .

186) The most desperate act of my life was when . . .

187) The most cunning thing I ever did was . . .

188) My most noble act was the time that I . . .

189) My greatest defeat was when . . .

190) The most fortunate thing that has
     ever happened to me was . . .

191) The most vivid memory of my childhood is . . .

192) The most hurtful criticism I ever received was . . .

193) The most despairing moment of my life was when . . .

194) I believe that when I die I will . . .

195) Ten things I want to do before I die are . . .

196) The most heroic thing I have ever done is . . .

197) Heaven is . . .

198) Hell is . . .

199) The worst betrayal of my life was when . . .

200) I will feel vindicated when . . .

201) I can hardly wait for . . .

202) I shouldn't think this, but . . .

203) One thing I cannot accept is . . .

204) I struggle to forgive _____ for _____ . . .

205) I am waiting for . . .

206) I can no longer wait for . . .

THE STORY-STRUCTURE QUESTIONS

In building your story, you are moving from the general to the specific. It is important to understand that you are not "plotting out" your story, but merely becoming more familiar with the key stages in your protagonist's journey. It is through exploring your protagonist's experiences that the plot emerges.

Write for five minutes (stream of consciousness) on these questions.

ACT ONE

1. Beginning: What is the mood, time, and place in which my memoir exists?
2. Dramatic Question: What is the dilemma at the heart of my memoir?
3. Inciting Incident: What event happens that sets my story into motion?
4. Opposing argument: What is the opposing argument to the Inciting Incident? Is there some kind of antagonistic response to my protagonist?
5. End of Act One: What decision does my protagonist make that they can't go back on? Where is there reluctance in this decision?

ACT TWO

6. False Hope: Where does my protagonist experience success or false hope as the result of making their decision?
7. Midpoint: What event happens that forces my protagonist to commit fully to their goal? How does this moment involve temptation for the protagonist? They could go back to where they were in the beginning or forge into the unknown and risk

losing everything.

8. Suffering: What does it look like when my protagonist realizes that this is more difficult than they had imagined? Do they consider giving up? What does it look like when they suffer? Do you see how the dilemma is becoming conscious?

9. Surrender: What does it look like when my protagonist realizes that what they wanted is impossible to achieve based on their current approach, or their current identity?

ACT THREE

10. Reality: What is the truth of my protagonist's reality that they finally accept? How does this galvanize them to take action?

11. Action: What action does my protagonist take toward getting what they need?

12. Battle Scene: What happens when my protagonist's want and need collide? What choice does my protagonist make?

13. New Equilibrium: What is the final image in my story? What does it look like when my protagonist is returned home? How are they relating differently to other characters? What have they come to understand?

PART FIVE

creating an outline

OVERVIEW OF THE KEY STAGES IN YOUR PROTAGONIST'S JOURNEY

ACT ONE

Opening/False Belief

Your protagonist wants something. Without a powerful want, there is no story. Until you have a sense of what your protagonist wants, you will be unclear on the engine that is driving your narrative. Your protagonist also carries with them a false belief, a mistaken idea of themselves and/or their world. Since the purpose of transformation is to reveal a wider perspective, the story often begins with a false belief that is founded on a set of incontestable facts, but as the story progresses, the interpretation of these facts evolves. For instance, in Cormac McCarthy's *The Road*, the man believes that the world is unsafe and that he must destroy anyone who crosses his path. In fact he is prepared to kill his own son if he perceives that the boy might suffer at the hands of another. And he is right. The world is a post apocalyptic nightmare, yet in the end the father is dead and a family happens upon the boy and takes him into their fold. It most certainly is a dark and terrifying world but it is not without hope as the father initially believed.

Dilemma

Your protagonist's desire is wrapped up in a false belief about what their goal actually means, which creates a dilemma. This dilemma is often called the dramatic problem of the story because it appears that they have a problem but in fact they have a dilemma. For example, a character may want love because they believe it will complete them. Through the story they may learn that their desire for love actually prevents them from ever having it. As long as they believe that they require a partner in order to feel complete, they will be unable to accept that their sense of wholeness comes from within. By introducing the protagonist's apparent "problem" early in the story, we understand the theme, i.e. the nature of their struggle in universal terms.

Inciting Incident

This is sometimes called the *"Why is this day unlike any other?"* moment. Whether it is Toto being taken away in *The Wizard of Oz* or Katniss' sister being chosen as a "tribute" in *The Hunger Games*, something happens that causes your protagonist to respond, thus providing a context for the dilemma.

Opposing Argument

This is a moment about two-thirds of the way through Act One where an antagonist responds to your protagonist thus presenting the other side of the "apparent" problem. This moment is necessary because it illustrates the protagonist's specific dilemma. Until our reader understands the nature of the dilemma, as opposed to the appearance of the problem, there will be no context for the protagonist's decision at the end of Act One. Conversely, it is only as a result of the Inciting Incident that the opposing argument can be understood.

Decision

At the end of Act One your protagonist makes a decision they can't go back on toward achieving their goal. This decision may involve anything from telling a secret, to proclaiming your love, to a first kiss, to moving across town, to accepting a promotion, to entering a wizardry academy. But remember, it's not simply about what happens, but rather the meaning we ascribe to what happens, that keeps our reader connected to your story. Therefore, pay special attention to the reluctance that comes with your protagonist's decision. This reluctance will help to dramatize the stakes your protagonist is facing. When Romeo sneaks into Juliet's compound and professes his love under her balcony he is certainly not indifferent towards her; however, his reluctance at the consequences of being discovered (her father could kill him) illustrates the danger of his action. Without reluctance, we will not have a context for your protagonist's dilemma.

ACT TWO

False Hope

At this point in the story, your protagonist achieves an initial success towards achieving their goal. Success appears to be within reach. Without this moment we do not have a context for the meaning they are making out of their goal. They are yet unaware of the conundrum besetting them. Consider Cyrano de Bergerac; if Cyrano's desire is to be loved by Roxanne, and he has succeeded in getting her to fall in love with his words through someone else, he has yet to confront his true dilemma which may be the meaning that he has made from that love. They have an idea of what their success should look like, but until they shed the meaning they have attached to it, they will be in bondage to their goal.

Midpoint – Temptation

As a result of your protagonist's false hope, an event happens that causes your protagonist to respond through temptation. They are pulled in two different directions between what they want and what they need. They have come a long way and have made great strides, but now are faced with a crisis of conscience. They can take a shortcut or they can risk everything for their dream.

Suffering

As you move into the second half of Act Two, the stakes are rising and they reach a point where they experience true suffering, a moment when they had no idea it was going to be this difficult and they entertain the notion of giving up. If they had known it was going to be this difficult, they would probably never have set out on this journey. The suffering is a direct result of your protagonist's dawning suspicion that what they want is impossible to achieve, based upon the meaning they have attached to their goal. In other words, they sense that what they are facing is not a problem, but rather a dilemma which is impossible to solve. The suffering is the death rattle of your protagonist's old identity. They're going to give it one last try.

Surrender

Your protagonist surrenders when they have run out of choices. The end of Act Two is where your protagonist recognizes the impossibility of ever achieving their goal, and they let it go. The end of Act Two is like a coin with two sides. On one side is the dark night of the soul, and on the other side is a wider perspective. This is where they reframe their relationship to their goal.

ACT THREE

Accepting Reality

By reframing their relationship to their goal, your protagonist accepts the *reality* of their situation as opposed to the *appearance* of their situation. This is where the meaning shifts. For example, if your protagonist's cry into the void is, "I've failed," they begin to accept that all of their attempts at succeeding were perhaps misguided, and they let go of their old definitions of success and failure. There's a saying: The truth will set you free but first it will kick your butt. That is where your protagonist is at this point. They are getting their butt kicked, but it is leading them to a new understanding of how things really work.

Action

This is the bulk of your third act. As a result of your protagonist accepting the reality of their situation, they take action towards giving themselves what they need as opposed to what they want. It doesn't mean that they've surrendered their outward desire, but only the meaning they've made out of it. They've come to recognize that they can no longer hold out hope that their desire will provide them with their true inner need, thus they take action towards fulfilling their heart's desire while knowing it may cost them everything they initially thought they wanted.

Battle Scene

This is the climax of your story where your protagonist makes a choice between what they want and what they need. This is an extremely difficult choice for your protagonist. Through this choice they prove to the gods that they have earned their transformation, and thus resolved their dilemma.

New Equilibrium

This is the ending of your story where your protagonist is returned home. How are they relating differently to the other characters in the story? What have they come to understand through their journey? It is important to find a way to dramatize this experience through action. It isn't enough to say that a character lives happily ever after. We must understand specifically what that means.

OUTLINE WORKSHEETS

ACT ONE
Opening/False Belief

Dilemma

Inciting Incident

Opposing Argument

Your Protagonist Makes a Decision

ACT TWO
Your Protagonist Experiences False Hope

Midpoint: Your Protagonist Experiences Temptation

Your Protagonist Suffers

Your Protagonist Surrenders

ACT THREE
Your Protagonist Accepts the Reality of Their Situation

Your Protagonist Takes Action

The Battle Scene

Your Protagonist Returns Home

PART SIX

sample outlines

Wild by Cheryl Strayed

Cheryl Strayed's powerful memoir *Wild* explores her journey in reclaiming her life after the loss of her mother. It examines the experience of being orphaned as an adult woman and her lapses into extramarital affairs and heroin use. In a final bid to free herself, with virtually no hiking experience she sets out on a solo journey through the Pacific Crest Trail. It is a powerful, heartbreaking, and redemptive story on the lengths we will go to find ourselves.

What follows are my personal notes on how she structured her memoir, including some thoughts on process. These are simply my observations. The thing to remember with story structure is that it is not the events themselves but rather the meaning we ascribe to the events that provides the scenes with meaning.

As I'll be referring to page numbers, all my notes are based on the Random House Vintage Books paperback edition.

ACT ONE

Establishing the World (page 3)

"The trees were tall, but I was taller." Nice opening line. Notice how the first sentence implies that this is a story of transformation. It also ignites our curiosity. Something has happened. What is it? We need to find out. Also, was this the first line she wrote in her first draft? Doubtful, right? Don't waste your time trying to write a great opening line before doing anything else. You will discover it as you write your first draft.

A common device in memoir is to begin with a crisis moment, an event that occurs much later in the narrative. It is often the end of Act Two (the dark night of the soul). It's a device to hook the reader, to cause them to wonder how on earth they will overcome this obstacle. The *Wild* prologue ends with Cheryl barefoot in the wilderness, miles from civilization. The final line is the solution to her problem, both real and metaphorical: *"Keep Walking."*

Theme/Dilemma (page 3–6)
Notice how we're experiencing Cheryl's dilemma from the very beginning. In order to find herself, she will hike the Pacific Crest Trail . . . which she might not survive. Forced to walk barefoot, she recounts for us how she got on the trail: traumatic childhood, mother has recently died (four years ago), stepfather has vanished, her family has become fractured, her marriage has crumbled after multiple affairs, and she's awash in despair and self-loathing. This is her final attempt to find herself. Notice how the dilemma is personal to her, but universal to the reader. *Will I survive the journey back to self?*

Inciting Incident (page 27)
Cheryl decides to trek the PCT. Her destination: The Bridge of the Gods. Now the reader knows what her goal is. She must get there or she will be lost forever.

Notice how she didn't begin with this goal. First, she set up her situation so we experienced why she had to go on this journey. Until we've experienced your protagonist's dilemma, there will be no context for the inciting incident.

Opposing Argument (page 75)
This is where Cheryl's dilemma becomes apparent. A man says, *"It's one thing to be a woman crazy enough to do what you're doing. Another thing to be a man letting his own wife go off and do this."*

She has lied to this man in order to protect herself, and is terrified of being assaulted. Will she survive this journey?

Notice how she has found a way to dramatize this question. It's not enough to tell us that the journey will be difficult. She has found an antagonistic force to experience the very real threat she is facing.

Decision/Reluctance (page 101)
Flashback: Cheryl ends her marriage. She says goodbye to the illusion of security. She is alone now, with no one to blame, and no one to hold onto. She decides to start her life over again. She changes her last name. (Great metaphor!)

But notice the reluctance around this decision. While she is finally free and living authentically, she must now confront her demons.

Notice also how the author jumps back and forth in time, using a flashback as a structural story point. Do you see how structure doesn't need to be chronological? As readers, we want to experience your protagonist making a decision and the reluctance around that decision. How you do that is entirely up to you.

ACT TWO

False Hope (page 135)
Notice how she is beginning to grow and adjust to this new environment. We're beginning to experience a sense that she just might be on her way to mastering this terrain.

"I had only just begun. I was three weeks into my hike, but everything in me felt altered. I lay in the water as long as I could without breathing, alone in a strange new land, while the actual world all around me hummed on."

There's a sense that she's going to be okay. In fact, there's a moment where it almost feels like the story could end. However, there are worthy antagonists lurking around the corner, inner demons that must be confronted. Notice the growth at this point compared to the beginning of the story. This is perhaps the first time in the story that she has felt hopeful.

Midpoint/Temptation (page 174)

Wild is somewhat of a picaresque memoir, with Cheryl meeting various characters along the way, each of whom plays a role in her ultimate transformation.

She meets Brent, a sweet and handsome younger man on the trail.

"I didn't want to say goodbye to him the next morning."

"Make a wish. It's our last night in the Sierra Nevada."

There's no going back. *"Goodbye Ranger of Light,"* I said to the sky.

Notice in your memoir where there might be a point of no return. Cheryl literally comes out and tells the reader, *"There's no going back."* Notice how she is taking us directly into the experience that pushes us into the second half of the book.

Suffering (page 204–205)

Cheryl meets an astrologer and tells us: *"She also said bizarrely specific things that were so accurate and particular, so simultaneously consoling and upsetting, that it was all I could do not to bawl in recognition and grief."*

"Your father was wounded. And you're wounded in the same place."

Notice how she is realizing that there is no escaping her past. She will always carry her wounds with her. She has lost her boots. Her feet are in agony. But more than that, they are merely an outward manifestation of the inner anguish she can never simply walk off. She is beginning to question why she ever set out on this journey to begin with. She is considering giving up.

"I put on my stupid sandals and began the long walk to Castle Crags."

The false hope she experienced early on in Act Two is being replaced by the grim fact that she can never outrun her grief. And that is what this memoir is about — the courage to grieve the past in order to build a new future. Cheryl is arriving at a truth. The dilemma is becoming apparent. No matter how far she walks or what she does, she can never escape herself or become a better version of herself. What began as journey to get somewhere else has led her to the place where she must finally stop and go within.

"The sight of the churned, barren earth unsettled me. I felt sad and angry about it, but in a way that include the complicated truth of my own complicity. I used tables and chairs and toilet paper too, after all.

. . . I wanted to have a family again."

Surrender (page 222–234)
As we approach the moment of surrender, Cheryl tells us, "*Sometimes it seemed that the Pacific Crest Trail was one long mountain I was ascending. That at my journey's end at the Columbia River, I'd reach the trail's summit, rather than its lowest point. This feeling of ascension wasn't only metaphorical. It literally felt as if I were almost always, impossibly, going up.*"

On page 231, she has met a five-year-old boy and his grandmother. They have a conversation and it comes out that the boy has been abandoned by his father and that his mother has died. And then the boy offers to sing her a song. It's Red River Valley.

"*Thank you,*" I said, half demolished by the time he finished. "*That might be the best thing I've ever heard in my whole life.*"

The appearance of this boy arrives at a critical point — his innocence and his unspeakable loss suddenly give context to Cheryl's own pain. It doesn't diminish her pain but it gives her permission to feel it. It's almost as if she owes it to the child.

She reflects on the loss of her own father, on his inability to father her the way she needed to be fathered, and she allows herself to grieve.

"*I laughed with the joy of it, and the next moment I was crying my first tears on the PCT. I cried and I cried and I cried. I wasn't crying because I was happy. I wasn't crying because I was sad. I wasn't crying because of my mother or my father or Paul. I was crying because I was full.*"

ACT THREE

Reality (page 233 – page 234)

Act Three often begins with the appearance of a gift. It can be a physical gift or simply the gift of insight. In *Wild*, a gift appears — she gets a new pair of boots. Notice how, by letting go of what she wants, which is some kind of existential salve to heal her broken spirit, a wider perspective appears and she begins to see her situation in a new way.

She accepts the truth of her situation as opposed to the appearance of her situation. She can never outrun her pain. And ironically, her boots arrive. She must keep going but her load is getting lighter. She's no longer demanding answers of the trail. She is simply allowing herself to be.

Notice as she reflects on her father's abandonment. *"It occurred to me that I didn't have to be amazed anymore."*

Notice this line at the end of the chapter. *"I was entering. I was leaving. California streamed behind me like a long silk veil. I didn't feel like a big fat idiot. I didn't feel like a hard-ass motherfucking Amazonian queen. I felt fierce and humble and gathered up inside, like I was safe in this world too."*

But the story isn't over here. The stakes continue to rise in Act Three. As a result of letting go of what she wants and accepting the reality of her situation, Cheryl takes action towards giving herself what she needs.

Action (page 265)

The action section is the bulk of your third act.

Notice that in giving herself what she needs, Cheryl begins to go to places she never allowed herself to go before. She commits heresy by raging at her beloved dead mother. She allows herself to feel the feelings she has never allowed herself to feel before. She is coming into her body. Reentry is messy and terrifying and liberating. She is accepting her mother, her stepfather, her brother, and her ex-husband as human, neither greater nor less than her. She is accepting her perfectly imperfect self. She is no longer running from her pain.

Notice on page 269 how Cheryl reflects back to her mother's dying days. It's a conversation with her mother about what to do with her body when she's dead. *"I want everything that can be donated to be donated,"* says her mother.

But Cheryl is relentless. *"What would you like to do with . . . what's . . . left over. Do you want to be buried or cremated?"*

"Burn me," she said finally. "Turn me to ash."

Notice how we are nearing the end of the story, and the author is giving us a flashback. There are no rules. Your memoir need not be chronological and while it's important to limit exposition in your third act, I think this scene is an exception that proves the rule. This experience takes us to the heart of Cheryl's grief, offering us a visceral image of her mother being burned to ashes.

Notice how this scene could theoretically have been placed in the beginning of the story. Her mother's death precedes her journey on the PCT, but she saves this for Act Three. There's an emotional wallop that happens here, a different meaning that is being expressed, a crucible of sorts that is happening as we approach the climax.

As we are galloping towards the climax, we experience a shift where the author is leaving her rational self behind and returning to some primordial self, returning to the earth as if she is attempting to reunite with her mother. There's a shocking moment where she remembers taking the remains of her mother, the largest pieces, and *"I put her burnt bones in my mouth and swallowed them whole."*

In the final few pages prior to the battle scene, Cheryl finds herself confronting predatory men. There is a savage sense of dread that everything in the story, every potential threat she has navigated up to this point has led us here. It is terrifying as she quietly negotiates her way to safety.

Battle Scene (page 299)

This is the climactic moment where all intellectual notions of a re-union are gone and Cheryl makes the difficult choice to let go of her mother, her past, her old life. It is a purging, a crucible, and its power is not simply in the words that happen here, but in all that has preceded it. Everything in the story leads to this moment and the moment is unadorned, almost anticlimactic in its simplicity, and yet its power arrives with the weight of all that has preceded it. The difficult choice is simply to accept herself as she is.

"Very nice," he said.

"What is?" I asked, turning to him, though I knew.

"Everything," he said.

And it was true.

New Equilibrium (309–311)

"I had arrived. I'd done it. It seemed like such a small thing and such a tremendous thing at once, like a secret I'd always tell myself, though I didn't know the meaning of it just yet. I stood there for several minutes, cars and trucks going past me, feeling like I'd cry, though I didn't."

Cheryl has arrived at her destination and as T.S. Eliot said, *"the end of all our exploring will be to arrive where we started and know the place as if for the first time."* Nothing much has changed for Cheryl. She is the same person. Outwardly, her circumstances are the same. She's still single and broke. Her relationships to the people in her life are essentially unchanged, and yet we know that she will never go back to the person she was before. Heroin, infidelities, and self-harm are now a thing of the past. She has grieved her losses and she has reclaimed herself.

In the final pages she summarizes her life going forward, an epilogue of sorts, where we experience her years later, getting married in a spot not far from the Bridge of the Gods, her destination. She is married now, with children, and she has found a freedom that she never previously imagined as a result of coming to accept herself fully.

Howl by Allen Ginsberg

Okay, here's an interesting exercise. I frequently get writers coming into the workshop who interpret story structure as a rule or a formula rather than what it is, which is an immutable paradigm for an inner transformation. (Remember, the purpose of story is to reveal a transformation.) It seems, as human beings, that there are a series of experiences we always pass through in our journey toward this shift in perception.

So just for fun, let's examine Allen Ginsberg's *Howl*, an experimental poem from the 1960s. (Just Google *Howl poem* and it will pop up.) While it is not technically a memoir, it is a memory and reflection on the time Ginsberg spent in a mental institution with his friend Carl Solomon.

In *Howl*, Ginsberg's irreverence merges the sacred with the profane as he takes us on an inner spiritual quest from existential despair to an almost ecstatic freedom. My hope is that if we can identify the key experiences in an experimental poem, then we can disabuse ourselves of the notion that story structure has much to do with the plotting of events but rather is a way to dramatize a series of internal experiences that leads to a transformed state.

Firstly, notice how this poem is written in *three parts*. This impulse, whether conscious or not, is a useful framing device, a way of codifying experiences into a series of relatable parts. Notice the different *parts* of our human journey: birth, life, death. Story is a circle — it involves the completion of a theme. Or, more accurately, it is a spiral and with each consecutive cycle, we are transported and hopefully understand our circumstances in a clearer way. Just look at the change of seasons to see the cycle of life, look at the ocean tides, or the movement of the earth as it revolves around the sun, creating morning, noon, and night. The three-act structure is encoded in our DNA; it is embedded in our psyche. It is a universal tool to understand and make meaning of our existence.

The first section of *Howl* is the longest, more than twice the length of Sections Two and Three. Therefore, in terms of proportion, I would argue that it takes us up to the midpoint.

Let's explore.

ACT ONE

Establishing the World

Here's the opening line: "*I saw the best minds of my generation destroyed by madness, starving hysterical naked, dragging themselves through the negro streets at dawn looking for an angry fix.*"

Notice that the poem begins by establishing the world. In this one line he has set the mood. There's a wild almost feral quality to his words. And it raises a question. What happened? Why did they go mad?

Theme/Dilemma

And following this, Ginsberg begins to answer the question by dramatizing their dilemma: "*. . . who passed through universities with radiant cool eyes hallucinating Arkansas and Blake-light tragedy among the scholars of war.*"

This seems to be a poem about institutions and the dilemma of institutional thinking, i.e. how the desire to be accepted by the former generation's *scholars of war* could cost them their individuality. In other words: conform or die. These bright minds, alive with curiosity and thoughts of peace and love, are colliding with the academic jingoism of the "Greatest Generation" who hold the keys to the corridors of power. Will their defiance cost them a place at the table?

Inciting Incident

Yes. They are not accepted. The very next line introduces a possible inciting incident: *". . . who were expelled from the academies for crazy & publishing obscene odes on the windows of the skull."*

While attempting to express themselves, the best minds have been pathologized or worse, dismissed — their deepest thoughts have been ridiculed and rejected. They've been deemed crazy.

Opposing Argument

Now the stakes are rising. The problem at the inciting incident, i.e., being thrown out for expressing their truth, has led to disillusionment. The opposing argument is where there's an antagonistic response to the protagonist's desire. The antagonist is the institution, the system that has denied them their truth. And now they're frightened and losing their minds. *". . . who cowered in unshaven rooms in underwear, burning their money in wastebaskets and listening to the Terror through the wall . . ."*

Notice that the protagonist(s) are going mad as the result of this rejection. Can they trust themselves? Should they conform or rebel? They are children, unformed. Will they make it in the adult world? Will they survive their rebellion, or will it cost them their souls?

". . . who created great suicidal dramas on the apartment cliff-banks of the Hudson under the wartime blue floodlight of the moon & their heads shall be crowned with the laurel of oblivion . . ."

How will they respond to this rejection?

Decision

Okay, they will rebel. Ginsberg goes on a long riff here, articulating the response to being rejected by the establishment by fighting the establishment.

". . . who burned cigarette holes in their arms protesting the narcotic tobacco haze of Capitalism, who distributed Supercommunist pamphlets in Union Square weeping and undressing while the sirens of Los Alamos wailed them down . . ."

". . . who bit detectives in the neck and shrieked with delight in

policecars for committing no crime but their own wild cooking ped-erasty and intoxication . . ."

Notice the decision to rebel. And notice the reluctance that comes with this decision. The reluctance comes in the acknowl-edgement that there are consequences to this rebellion, i.e., self-harm, incarceration.

ACT TWO

False Hope

But damn it, it's also fun, at least for a while. It's an escape from the stultifying boredom of the ruling class.

". . . who hiccuped endlessly trying to giggle but wound up with a sob behind a partition in a Turkish Bath when the blond & naked angel came to pierce them with a sword . . ."

Midpoint/Temptation

But the protagonist's rebellion is taking a toll. They are lost, direc-tionless, unclear on the nature of their rebellion. It seemed they were fighting a system but the system has becoming increasingly abstract. Perhaps their rebellion is more existential than they imag-ined. Regardless, their restlessness has turned to vice, addiction in a variety of forms. Conformity hasn't worked, nor has rebellion. Now our protagonist(s) are lost and facing a moment of temptation.

". . . to recreate the syntax and measure of poor human prose and stand before you speechless and intelligent and shaking with shame, rejected yet confessing out the soul to conform to the rhythm of thought in his naked and endless head, the madman bum and angel beat in Time, unknown, yet putting down here what might be left to say in time come after death . . ."

This is the midpoint, their point of no return. The story moves in a new direction. In an about face, they turn *toward* an institution to save them, thus the dilemma persists. In saving their lives, will it cost them their souls?

". . . ah, Carl, while you are not safe I am not safe, and now you're really in the total animal soup of time . . ."

In an attempt to connect to themselves, it leads to self-disgust, self-abandonment, disconnection, and despair.

And we arrive at the final line of Section One: "*. . . with the absolute heart of the poem of life butchered out of their own bodies good to eat a thousand years.*"

Notice that an event has happened (they are experiencing the possibility of a soul death).

Notice the temptation — submitting to the institution might cost them their soul.

But nonetheless, they enter the asylum.

Suffering

The second half of Act Two begins with Section Two of the poem: "*What sphinx of cement and aluminum bashed open their skulls and ate up their brains and imagination?*"

Now we are in the mental institution with a lament to Moloch: "*Moloch! Solitude! Filth! Ugliness! Ashcans and unobtainable dollars!*"

In the Hebrew bible, Moloch was a fallen angel, a demonic creature that masqueraded as a pagan fertility god with an appetite for fire sacrifices of children by the parents of the faithful. In Section Two, virtually every line begins with a cry to Moloch. The best minds of the generation are now experiencing a new struggle. In order to survive, they have entered the belly of the beast. Moloch is represented in a variety of ways: "*Moloch whose mind is pure machinery! . . . Moloch whose eyes are a thousand blind windows!*"

If the eyes are the windows to the soul, then the soul is invisible to this institution. This is where the dilemma is becoming apparent. "*They broke their backs lifting Moloch to Heaven!*" It is as if, in their misguided attempts to be free, they are attempting to resurrect a demon rather than exorcising it. They are waking up to the impossibility of ever achieving their goal, based on their current approach. They are recognizing the impossibility of ever reconciling with their oppressors.

Surrender

The second section is relatively short and the lament's tone doesn't change much, but it leads us to a dark night of the soul. The final line of this section reads: *"They jumped off the roof! to solitude! waving! carrying flowers! Down to the river! into the street!"*

They have recognized the impossibility of ever being seen and heard by the establishment. The system is not equipped to process individuals. And so they let go. And they escape back to the streets.

ACT THREE

Reality

But something has shifted. While they are still mad, they have let go. They are still lost but they are beginning to glimpse their North Star. Yes, they have gone mad but they are not alone. And perhaps madness is getting redefined here. Perhaps it means connection, passion, life!

Action

As we move into the final section, it begins: *"Carl Solomon! I'm with you in Rockland, where you're madder than I am."*

Rockland is the mental institution from which Ginsberg has emerged but where his friend Carl Solomon still remained. Every line in this section begins with *"I'm with you in Rockland."*

This is the beating heart of Act Three. Our protagonist(s) appear to have let go of what they want; i.e. acceptance and approval from the establishment — and are finding a connection with each other.

Rather than running in shame from our madness, perhaps it is something to be celebrated. This is the work of Act Three, to integrate the two opposing forces of the dramatic question which is: the individual versus the institution.

"I'm with you in Rockland where you bang on the catatonic piano the soul is innocent and immortal it should never die ungodly in an armed madhouse . . ."

It is as if Ginsberg is fighting for his friend from afar. Having entered the institution, Ginsberg has recognized that the institution was a paper tiger and that his desire to be accepted was the very thing that was preventing him from achieving his goal. The external system is broken, and so, he will connect to the internal system within him — his heart, his humanity.

He is waking up to his truth as an artist and a poet, as a free thinker. He is integrating the two aspects of himself that he alluded to from the beginning, the "great mind" and the "madman" and is making room for both of them.

Battle Scene

The penultimate line is where the difficult choice is made.

"I'm with you in Rockland where we wake up electrified out of the coma by our own soul's airplanes roaring over the roof they've come to drop angelic bombs the hospital illuminates itself — imaginary walls collapse — O skinny legions run outside — O starry-spangled shock of mercy the eternal war is here — O victory forget your underwear we're free."

The difficult choice is to accept oneself fully, the great mind of a generation, along with the madness, the shame, the confusion, the terrible baggage of having to be a human in a world run by institutions. The struggle continues but we're arriving at a new place here where we know there is no going back, where we trust that together these mad minds will prevail because they are united.

They have let go of searching outside of themselves for acceptance and validation. They have rejected the institutions and academies of higher learning in favor of their heart's desire.

New Equilibrium

And finally, our protagonist returns home. It's interesting that the poem moves from the general to the specific. While it's probably safe to assume that Ginsberg is included in the line about "*the great minds of my generation,*" the protagonist here has become singular.

"I'm with you in Rockland in my dreams you walk dripping from a sea-journey on the highway across America in tears to the door of my cottage in the Western night."

The poem ends with tears (the character has been returned to their feelings) as the journey across America comes to an end in what feels like a physical embrace.

ACKNOWLEDGMENTS

Thank you to my editor and tireless assistant, Katharine Chezum. I am so grateful for all that you do. Your thoroughness and patience are such a gift, and I really should tell you that every day. Thank you to Eric Lynxwiler for doing such a beautiful job on the interior book design. Thank you to Amy Inouye for doing the book covers for the 90-Day series — it was such a pleasure working with you. Enjoy your well-deserved retirement. I will miss you.

Thanks to Mindi White's keen eye for proofing the manuscript — I had no idea I was so comma obsessed. Thank you to my posse, Giuseppe, Ral and Steve, for your love and friendship over the decades, and to Bill Barnett for your wisdom and insight.

To my dear wife Mary-Beth, this would be a different book without your input and compassionate eye. I hope I have absorbed some of your love and generosity, and that it has found its way onto these pages. You've taught me what it means to be part of a family. And to our son, Ray, for being you so completely.

Finally, thank you to my students over these last few decades for your courage, and for always pushing me towards the truth. *The 90-Day Memoir* explores many facets of the craft, but I believe it comes down to this: *Memoir is simply the act of dramatizing the journey to self-love.* Always remember that it is safe to trust yourself.

FREE 90-DAY MEMOIR RESOURCES

For free resources to support you with your 90-day memoir, including a story structure meditation video, downloadable worksheets, sample outlines and an ongoing library of videos, please go to **lawriterslab.com/resources**.

TAKE THE 90-DAY MEMOIR WORKSHOP LIVE

For more information on my LIVE online 90-Day Memoir workshop, or to receive my free monthly newsletter, please go to **lawriterslab.com**.

Made in the USA
Coppell, TX
02 April 2024

30835218R00198